The Miracle of

FAITH GOALS

*How to achieve 100 to 1,000
times more in your life*

DAVE WILLIAMS

THE MIRACLE OF FAITH GOALS

How to achieve 100 to 1,00 times more in your life

Unless otherwise noted, all Scripture quotations are taken from the *King James Version* of the Bible.

Scriptures marked CEV are taken from the *Contemporary English Version*® Copyright © 1995. Used by permission of American Bible Society. All rights reserved.

Scripture quotations marked NLT are taken from the *Holy Bible, New Living Translation*, copyright © 1996, 2004. Used by permission of Tyndale House Publishers, Inc., Wheaton, Illinois, 60189. All rights reserved.

Scriptures marked MSG are taken from *The Message*®. Copyright © 1993, 1994, 1995, 1996, 2000, 2001, 2002. Used by permission of NavPress Publishing Group.

Scripture quotations marked AMP are taken from the *Amplified*® *Bible*, Copyright © 1954, 1958, 1962, 1964, 1965, 1987 by The Lockman Foundation. Used by permission. (www.Lockman.org)

Copyright © 2013 by Dr. David R. Williams
Cover designed by Kristy Prince

ISBN 978-0-938020-61-5

DP
DECAPOLIS
PUBLISHING

Printed in the United States of America

Books by Dave Williams

ABC's of Success and Happiness
Angels: They are Watching You
Beatitudes: Success 101
The Beauty of Holiness
Coming Into the Wealthy Place
The Desires of Your Heart
Developing the Spirit of a Conqueror
Elite Prayer Warriors
Emerging Leaders
End-Times Bible Prophecy
Filled
Genuine Prosperity
Gifts that Shape Your Life and Change Your World
Have You Heard from the Lord Lately?
How to Be a High Performance Believer
How to Help Your Pastor Succeed
The Jezebel Spirit
Miracle Breakthrough Power of the First Fruit
Miracle Results of Fasting
The New Life...The Start of Something Wonderful
Pacesetting Leadership
The Pastor's Pay
The Presence of God
Private Garden
Radical Fasting
Radical Forgiveness
Radical Healing
Regaining Your Spiritual Momentum
The Road to Radical Riches
Seven Sign Posts on the Road to Spiritual Maturity
Skill for Battle: The Art of Spiritual Warfare
Somebody Out There Needs You
Toxic Committees and Venomous Boards
What to Do if You Miss the Rapture
The World Beyond
Your Pastor: A Key to Your Personal Wealth
Your Spectacular Mind

TABLE OF CONTENTS

FOREWORD
BY JOHN O'LEARY

The dictionary defines game changer as *something that radically changes a situation* or a *person who is a visionary*. My definition is a little simpler: it is Pastor Dave Williams.

I remember the Sunday morning in January that Pastor Dave Williams began his series on setting faith goals. It was a message that would have a huge impact on me, not only on that day but also for years to come. As I reflect back on it, that teaching series was absolutely a game changer, transforming the way I think, act, speak, and dream.

Early in his message Dave challenged us with a question: "Can you articulate ten goals you currently have for your life?" He continued, "And please don't give me some wimpy answer like, 'I want world peace and a good life.' Give me real, concrete goals! Because you can't get to a place if you don't know where you are going."

He said it again. "You can't get to a place if you don't know where you are going!"

That message hit hard—really hard.

As a business owner, I am accustomed to casting a vision and setting the direction I want my business to take. But I have to admit I was struggling to come up with any tangible goals for my personal life, and the ones I did write were weak generalizations...I was the wimp!

Over the following weeks, I began to develop a list of goals for the coming year. I started with the Four F's (faith, family, finance, and fitness) and tried to be specific about what I would like to achieve in each of those areas. Once completed—with both my chest and head hugely inflated—I presented my list to my wife for review. Judy took one look and asked, "Where's the Faith? Most of these goals are achievable simply by working a little harder. I don't see any big dreams that call on God."

She was right!

I realized that my new goals were all within *my* control if I just applied myself. My dreams were small and my goals manageable. They weren't the faith-stretching, world-changing dreams Pastor Dave had called for.

I went back to the drawing board, dreamed bigger, applied the techniques Dave Williams had talked about, and revised my list. This time, my list didn't include regular goals at all; it was full of faith goals.

I played the "what if" game with myself. It's a fun game to play: you simply dream up some of the best possible outcomes for your life, and then try to one-up them. Ask yourself, "What if this could get even better?" At first it might seem difficult, but soon it becomes just plain fun.

Dave Williams has completely revolutionized my thinking! He has taught me to dream big and set big goals. I have learned how to make them specific and measurable. For example, one of the goals on my initial list was that my company be profitable. But I quickly realized that if we made one single dollar, we'd be considered profitable. Now, I look to the most profitable companies in our industry and use their numbers as a benchmark for my business.

One year I set a goal to be debt free, but then my wife reminded me that the homeless are debt free. Once again I redefined that goal—paying off my mortgage, cars, and credit cards—owning assets and owing no man anything.

The strategies you will discover in this book will help you become an expert at developing and fine-tuning your own set of faith goals.

These goals then become a road map to begin your journey. Let me share with you some of the places our road map has taken us:

- **Just three years from that first Sunday, my company experienced its most profitable year ever in our one hundred year history.**
- **Judy had a goal to fly first-class every time we travel. That same year, I was asked to serve on two company boards that required travel. Our frequent flyer status allowed us to be bumped to first-class on many of our flights.**
- **Judy and I have written and published a book.**
- **We have become public speakers.**

The list goes on and on, and it all started with a faith goal. Now it is your turn! The principles Dave Williams lays out in this book are powerful tools that will advance you to new levels of living. The strategies are proven, and the steps to begin are simple and straightforward. You will think bigger, you will dream bigger, and you will live bigger! Dave Williams continues to have a profound effect on my life. He is an *ultimate game changer!*

~ John O'Leary

Editor's Note: John O'Leary is president of **O'Leary Paint Company**, manufacturers of nation-ally acclaimed, award winning paints. He and his wife, Judy, are coauthors of the top selling book, *Upward: Strategies for Success in Business, Life, and Relationships.* For more information on O'Leary Paint, visit: www.olearypaint.com. The book *Upward* is available on Amazon Kindle, Barnes & Noble Nook, and at www.davewilliams.com.

Goals that are not coupled with genuine
faith can actually kindle a fire of
inner emptiness even when
they are achieved.

CHAPTER 1

GOALS & FAITH GOALS

I am so happy you have this book in your hands.

You are about to experience a divine transformation into peak achievement through the amazing practice of setting and reaching faith goals. Just as a jet fighter is catapulted off an aircraft carrier, your life is being positioned to catapult to new levels of intimacy with God, creativity, and high-level achievement.

My prayer is that the revelation found on these pages will move to your head and your heart, causing you to take some faith actions toward being more—and having more—than you previously ever dreamed possible.

I first conducted my **Faith Goals Seminar** in Nashville, Tennessee, several years ago. One of the attendees, Dale, became so inspired that not only did he immediately begin setting and reaching his own faith goals, but he also began sharing the miracle of faith goals with everyone he met—on the job, at a restaurant...everywhere.

When I saw Dale again, he told me that one man's sarcastic response was, "Oh, that goal-setting stuff. I've heard it for years. It doesn't work." But Dale quickly responded, "This isn't about goal setting! I'm not talking about regular goals. I'm talking about FAITH GOALS...and there's a huge difference!"

As you will see, *there is a difference between mere "goals" and "faith goals!"*

Goals are important, but goals alone, without faith, can end up being nothing but fantasies.

> [6] "Human life is but a breath, and it disappears like a shadow. Our struggles are senseless; we store up more and more, without ever knowing who will get it all.
>
> [7] "What am I waiting for? I depend on you, Lord!"
>
> **Psalm 39:6–7 CEV**

Goals that are not coupled with genuine faith can actually kindle a fire of inner emptiness even when they are achieved. Solomon discovered this when he achieved all his lofty goals, but left God out. He built huge homes, gardens, and cities. Yet he felt hollow after all his achievements. He reached all his goals but became cynical and frustrated—empty without the relationship with God he once enjoyed. He wrote:

> So I set out to learn everything from wisdom to madness and folly. But I learned firsthand that pursuing all this is like chasing the wind.
>
> **Ecclesiastes 1:17 NLT**

> [17] So I came to hate life because everything done here under the sun is so troubling. Everything is meaningless—like chasing the wind.
>
> [18] I came to hate all my hard work here on earth, for I must leave to others everything I have earned.
>
> [19] And who can tell whether my successors will be wise or foolish? Yet they will control everything I have gained by my skill and hard work under the sun. How meaningless!

20 So I gave up in despair, questioning the value of all my hard work in this world.

Ecclesiastes 2:17–20 NLT

Human goals alone can produce things that won't last because, as Jesus said, the flesh can only produce more flesh. But if your dreams, visions, and goals are born of the Spirit, they will be spirit. They will count for eternity and last forever.

That which is born of the flesh is flesh; and that which is born of the Spirit is spirit.

John 3:6

- Faith goals carry the astonishing power to transform your life, family, marriage, ministry, or business into an amazing and successful adventure.
- Faith goals furnish you with the power and means to achieve 100 to 1000 times more in perhaps half the time.
- Faith goals provide you with the opportunity for remarkable intimacy with God.
- Faith goals are rooted in the Bible.

Therefore I say unto you, What things soever ye desire, when ye pray, believe that ye receive them, and ye shall have them.

Mark 11:24

Now faith is the assurance (the confirmation, the title deed) of the things [we] hope for, being the proof of things [we] do not see and the conviction of their reality [faith perceiving as real fact what is not revealed to the senses]

Hebrews 11:1 AMP

> **So I run with purpose in every step. I am not just shadowboxing.**
>
> **1 Corinthians 9:26 NLT**

THE DIFFERENCE BETWEEN A "GOAL" AND A "FAITH GOAL"

Some sincere people set goals and work themselves into the grave trying to achieve them. They exert all their natural energies to accomplish these human-set targets. Quite often, when they do realize these goals, they experience a feeling of emptiness inside, a let-down and sense of dissatisfaction. Achieving goals on your own, by the "sweat of your brow," can leave you profoundly unfulfilled.

> **Are ye so foolish? having begun in the Spirit, are ye now made perfect by the flesh?**
>
> **Galatians 3:3**

Faith goals are different because, although they are goals, they are goals inspired by the dreams and visions God graciously puts on your heart during those lingering moments in his presence. Faith goals are goals where God works *with* you. When you reach them you can truly say, "Look what the Lord has done!"

> **Many will see what he has done and be amazed. They will put their trust in the LORD.**
>
> **Psalm 40:30 NLT**

When the Lord helps you reach your impressive faith goals, others will be amazed and decide to put their trust in the Lord too. So, in addition to providing you an exceptional life, the practice of setting and reaching faith goals functions as an instrument of inspiring others as well.

Human goals say, "Look what I have achieved." Faith goals say, "Look what the Lord has done!"

Human goals say, "You must work really hard to achieve this." Faith goals say, "You do your part, and let God do his!"

Human goals are achieved by human effort. Faith goals are achieved in a partnership with God.[1]

Human goals require human energy, exertion, and plenty of grunt work. Faith goals also require energy, but it's the inexhaustible energy of God's Spirit.[2]

WHY FAITH GOALS ARE MORE POWERFUL THAN HUMAN GOALS

Human goals are important and can be rewarding. Not all human goals lead to emptiness and frustration. When you are trying to accomplish an enormous task, instead of scattering your efforts on ineffective activities, a goal helps brings the single-mindedness and focus needed for the achievement.

But a faith-goal is even more powerful than a human goal, because faith goals are micro-steps that go into achieving a dream you believe God put in your heart. Faith goals have scriptural backing. They are not just something a person dreams up on his own. Goals are important. Faith goals are *really* important.

What happens when we have no faith goals? We drift, we become aimless like a ship that sets out to sea and then turns the engines off, hoping to drift someplace tropical. Well, I hope we drift to Hawaii or Fiji. The chances are pretty close to ZERO![3]

Stop and think. Isn't that the way many people live their lives? They just drift. Isn't that how many ministries and busi

---

[1] Isaiah 40:30–31
[2] Mark 16:20
[3] Romans 8:11

nesses are operating today? They just drift, hoping someday God will do something. And they do nothing to break down their macro picture into manageable segments we call micro-steps or faith goals.

WHY SOME NEVER GET WHAT THEY WANT

> **The fear of the wicked, it shall come upon him: but the desire of the righteous shall be granted.**
>
> **Proverbs 10:24**

The number one reason why people don't have what they want is because they don't *know* what they want. Most people have never intentionally articulated their dreams and aspirations or the things they really want. But once you learn what my students have learned in my **Faith Goals Seminar,**[4] you will see your life—step-by-step—becoming more extraordinary, fulfilled, and possibly skyrocketing to new dimensions of productivity.

SOME COMMENTS FROM MY STUDENTS:

"Wish I knew this stuff years ago. This has changed the way I think in so many ways and caused me to make decisions and choices differently."   —RW

"My thinking has been transformed and enlarged to look for opportunities, as well as believing God and his Word in a new way!"   —LW

"It literally changed the destiny of my family."   —JG

"This has been one of the best investments we have ever made."   —CS

"Since making my prayer-dream book, four of the things I listed have already come to pass."   —AW

"This has changed my life!"   —DO

---

[4] ***Faith Goals Seminar***, Dave Williams Ministries, www.davewilliams.com/faithgoals

WHAT IF YOU COULD ACHIEVE 100 TO 1,000 TIMES MORE?

What if I could show you a simple act of faith that could cause your productivity to soar by 100 to 1000 times?

What if this practice also carried the benefit of launching you into a deeper intimacy with your Creator?

What if you could give $100,000 or more each year for charitable and mission projects?

Have you thought about these things?

Stop and think for a moment about all the dreams you used to have. What stopped you from dreaming?

This book could be one of the most transformational books you've ever read. This may be the tool God uses to radically upgrade and enlarge your performance and launch you to fresh dimensions of influence and fulfillment. Let me be your coach for a season through these pages.

When I learned this little-known secret about faith goals, it transformed my life, ministry, family, income, charitable giving and personal net assets. It helped me understand that it's just as easy for God to send hundreds and thousands as it is for him to send ones and tens. Our church grew exponentially when I began to practice setting faith goals.

Our little church had never given more than $35,000 to missions in any given year. That was it! So I set a faith goal of giving $1,000,000 to missions every year and a target date to begin. And it actually happened one year before I had planned! When I left the pastorate after more than 30 years, our church was giving over $3,000,000 a year to missions. A CPA verified that over the course of 30 years, our church had given over $40,000,000 to mission's projects and ministries worldwide. God works with you when you express faith through setting faith goals.

The practice of setting faith goals is rooted in God's Word, so it's going to work!

Having goals is better than having no goals, but just setting a bunch of goals—without God working with you—will probably leave you unfulfilled when you achieve them. But there is no emptiness, disillusionment, or lack of fulfillment with faith goals, because they always include God working with you.

Yogi Berra, one of the greatest catchers in baseball history, once said, **"If you don't know where you're going, you might wind up someplace else."** And you probably will, because success, whether it's personal, ministerial, or professional depends on your willingness to take your macro-picture—your dream, your vision—and convert it into reality by using faith goals.

DESIGNING AN EXCEPTIONAL LIFE

Setting faith goals is the practice of cooperating with the Divine. It's partnering with God to design an exceptional life. A faith goal will give focus to faith.

You're about to do something failures never do. Fruitless, unproductive people never set faith goals. It never occurs to them that faith is the only thing that pleases God. It never occurs to them that faith is the substance of *the things you hope for*. It never occurs to them to believe Jesus when he said, "What things soever you desire, when you pray, believe that you receive them and you shall have them."[5]

Faith Goals are micro-steps that take you forward toward your macro-picture, the vision or dream God has put on your heart. Let's get started right away on designing your extraordinary future, by first learning about your values and your vision.

---

[5] Mark 11:24

V1 **Values:** Stemming from God's Word

V2 **Vision:** Your General Concept, Dream, or Desire

V3 **Voicing:** Making Your Faith Forecast

V4 **Vividness:** Setting Faith Goals, Plans, Organizing

V5 **Visioning:** Seeing it in Your Inner Person in Detail

V6 **Vitalizing:** Bringing Life to Faith Goals by Action

V7 **Victory:** Seeing Your Dream Realized

CHAPTER 2

HOW VALUES LEAD TO VISION

Faith goals are micro-steps that keep you walking toward your macro-picture (your vision or dream). Your vision will flow from your values. If it is outside of your values, it's not a *God* opportunity and will doubtlessly invite a great deal of frustration into your life.

Your vision (general dream) will flow from the Holy Spirit through your values. For example, if faith is your first value, and you are invited to speak at an event that prohibits you from mentioning your faith, you will probably add this opportunity to your not-to-do list.

Years ago the mayor of Lansing invited me to be the speaker for the city's Memorial Day service. I told him I would accept if I could talk about my faith in Jesus. He agreed...and so did I. Imagine that! At the conclusion of the service, I even invited people to pray the prayer of salvation and had the privilege to minister to some emotionally struggling Vietnam veterans. Afterward a senior city council woman hugged me and said,

"Pastor Williams, please don't ever leave Lansing. We need you!" After that event, I was invited to other city events to pray or speak.

When I was pastor of Mount Hope Church[1] in Lansing, we established general values, taken from the words of Jesus himself. Our top two values were:

1. Loving God

2. Loving People

> [30] And thou shalt love the Lord thy God with all thy heart, and with all thy soul, and with all thy mind, and with all thy strength: this is the first commandment.
>
> [31] And the second is like, namely this, Thou shalt love thy neighbour as thyself. There is none other commandment greater than these.
>
> Mark 12:30–31

Every vision, dream, plan, ministry, and program for our church flowed from those two top values.

THE INVISIBLE CREATES THE VISIBLE

It is the invisible that creates the visible. Working with God, arm-in-arm, we have an awesome creative power.

> Through faith we understand that the worlds were framed by the word of God, *so that things which are seen were not made of things which do appear.*
>
> Hebrews 11:3 italics added

> *While we look not at the things which are seen, but at the things which are not seen:* for the things which are seen are temporal; but the things which are not seen are eternal.
>
> 2 Corinthians 4:18 italics added

---

[1] Mount Hope Church, 202 S. Creyts Road, Lansing, MI, 48917. www.mounthopechurch.org

We'll discuss this further throughout the book. I personally have articulated seven of my most important values in life. During one of my faith goals seminars, a man said he puts fun before fitness and finances. That's okay. You have to express your own values. They don't have to be the same as mine, or in the same order of priority, but they may be.

1. My Faith
2. My Family
3. My Friends
4. My Fitness
5. My Finances
6. My Future
7. My Fun

My friend, Dr. Keith Johnson, in his book *The LQ Solution*[2] (leadership quotient) talks about a "not-to-do-list." By knowing and articulating your values, you have a built-in screening process for every so-called opportunity that comes to your life. If an activity, plan, or action does not fit with your values, you can immediately add it to your not-to-do list!

Why don't you stop now, and prayerfully write out your values below in the order of their priority. See if you can come up with seven top values in your life.

1. _____
2. _____
3. _____
4. _____
5. _____
6. _____
7. _____

[2] Johnson, Keith; *The LQ Solution*, (Amazon Digital Services, Inc., 2012).

THE V7 STRATEGY CAN "MIRACLE-IZE" YOUR LIFE

Let me introduce you to what I call **The V7 Strategy** for peak achievement. The V7 Strategy works like a flow chart.

- **Values:** are defined by meditating on what is important to you. Your values flow into vision...

- **Vision:** is an inner picture of what you want to see achieved in your life. Vision flows into voicing...

- **Voicing:** is when you begin talking about your vision and speaking aloud faith forecasts and declarations concerning it. Voicing flows into vividness...

- **Vividness:** brings your vision into clarity with planning, organizing, and setting faith goals. Vividness flows into visioning...

- **Visioning:** is *not* the same as vision. Visioning is when you *see* the end result inside you. Every day in prayer and at work or play, you dream it, feel it, and speak God's Word over it. Visioning flows into vitalizing...

- **Vitalizing:** is when you begin giving actual life to your vision. It's when you begin taking action steps, trusting God to do what only he can do.

- **Victory:** all six of these practices flow into number seven—victory! You have achieved and realized your dream.

> **Hope deferred makes the heart sick, but a dream fulfilled is a tree of life.**
>
> **Proverbs 13:12 NLT**

**It is pleasant to see dreams come true, but fools
refuse to turn from evil to attain them.**

Proverbs 13:19 NLT

THE V7 FLOW STRATEGY LOOKS LIKE THIS:

V1 **Values:** Stemming from God's Word

V2 **Vision:** Your General Concept, Dream, or Desire

V3 **Voicing:** Making Your Faith Forecast

V4 **Vividness:** Setting Faith Goals, Plans, Organizing

V5 **Visioning:** Seeing it in Your Inner Person in Detail

V6 **Vitalizing:** Bringing Life to Faith Goals by Action

V7 **Victory:** Seeing Your Dream Realized

In the next chapter, we'll look more closely at V2: your vision.

V1 **Values:** Stemming from God's Word

V2 **Vision:** Your General Concept, Dream, or Desire

V3 **Voicing:** Making Your Faith Forecast

V4 **Vividness:** Setting Faith Goals, Plans, Organizing

V5 **Visioning:** Seeing it in Your Inner Person in Detail

V6 **Vitalizing:** Bringing Life to Faith Goals by Action

V7 **Victory:** Seeing Your Dream Realized

CHAPTER 3

MIRACLE-IZE YOUR LIFE WITH A VISION

The prudent understand where they are going, but fools deceive themselves.

Proverbs 14:8 NLT

In this chapter we'll focus on V2: Vision. This is the subject that many people have the greatest difficulty understanding.

Years ago, I took part in a church growth conference. All the presenters talked about vision as if everyone understood the concept. Yet when it was Q & A time, the attendees had more questions about vision than anything else. At that time, Wayne Benson was pastor of the largest church in Michigan, and he addressed the conference in a brilliant manner:

> *"If I held an acorn in my hand and asked people what it was, most would say, 'It's nothing but a little acorn.' But the person of vision would look at it not as nothing but a little acorn. The person of vision would say, 'I see a mighty oak there in your hand.'"*

I would add that a person of greater vision would say, "I see a whole city filled with mighty oak trees there in your hand."

People with vision see things not as they are now, but as they shall be in the future.

WHAT DO I MEAN BY "VISION"?

Technically, a vision is a little different than a dream, so I'll define the two. For the sake of this study, however, I will use the terms "dream" and "vision" interchangeably because both represent the big picture of your desired future.

A vision is an inner image or concept of where you want to go from where you are now.

A dream is a personal aspiration, desire, hope, or wish. Dreams can be designed by the dreamer, in harmony with the Master's assignment for his or her life. For example, Nehemiah had a dream of rebuilding the wall around Jerusalem.

When I write about vision, I am not writing about an experience only for those on the outer edge of weirdness. I think we've all met people who claim to have a vision every few minutes. I believe in supernatural visions, but that's not what I'm referring to in this book. What I mean by vision is a comprehensive sense of the following:

- **Where you are now**
- **Where you are going**
- **The "big picture" of something in your future**
- **A concept of where you're headed with your life, your ministry, your business, and your family**

If you are willing to see the invisible, you can accomplish the impossible! Vision is the driving force behind all the actions and activities of every highly motivated team. Every member sees the end result. Vision is the characteristic that sets apart the real achievers and winners in life from the drifters and whiners in life.

You will be happy to learn that success is the result primarily of vision and faith goals—NOT of resources, support, or the approval of people.

Vision and faith goals will trump money, talent, and brains every time.

Pat Robertson had less than $80.00, but that didn't stop him. With just a dream, some faith goals, and supportive family and friends, he went on to build a world-class television network. It wasn't money or connections that did this. It was a vision and faith goals!

Oral Roberts will go down in history as one of the greatest achievers of all time. Thirty million people globally came to know Jesus Christ through Oral's ministry. When he started, all he had was $11.00 and a vision. He surrounded himself with people of knowledge, set faith goals, and obeyed God's prophetic word to his heart. With a word from God, a clear vision, and faith goals, no man could hold him back. He held campaigns around the world, and built a world-class university in spite of all the so-called "impossibilities."

St. Paul had a vision of a glorious church.[1] St. Peter had a vision of a church that would be like a structure made of living stones.[2]

THE TRAGEDY OF LIFE WITH NO VISION

In the third chapter of Samuel we read about a time in history when there was no open vision (shared vision). The result: everyone did what was right in his own eyes. This brought chaos to the nation and everybody came out losers!

[1] Ephesians 5:27
[2] 1 Peter 2:5

> ...Now in those days messages from the Lord were
> very rare, and visions were quite uncommon.
>
> **1 Samuel 3:1b NLT**

Businesspeople, pastors, CEO's, and other leaders consider me as their coach, or at least one of their coaches. I currently enjoy over 600 leaders in my personal coaching alliance.

Because of this, it's important that I stay current with business and ministry trends. I recently came upon a fascinating blog by a researcher who studies businesses and publishes his research. The blog captured my attention. Here's an excerpt from *Ten Reasons Why Businesses Fail.*[3]

> *"Lack of a vision of the desired future,
> communicated and understood by all employees.
> Every decision in the company should be viewed
> as to whether it helps to achieve the vision."*
>
> *"Lack of a good strategic plan. With the aid of
> the vision of the future state of the organization,
> a list of actions necessary to reach that vision is
> needed to guide activity."*

Without a vision, (the macro picture) people develop the tendency to allow little foxes that spoil the vine or hinder progress. Without a vision, a person typically will focus on minor, non-essential issues.

> **Our vineyards are in blossom; we must catch the
> little foxes that destroy the vineyards.**
>
> **Song of Solomon 2:15 CEV**

People with no vision often criticize the vision of others. They fight with one another over insignificant matters, like mu

---

[3] http://basicbusiness.areavoices.com/2012/07/05/ten-reasons-why-businesses-fail/

sic styles, puppets or no puppets for children's Sunday School, dress up or come casual—the list goes on and on.

Mike Myatt, wrote *"Businesses Don't Fail—Leaders Do"* in his excellent article in **Forbes**.[4] How do leaders fail? In his article, Mike described the biggest causes of failure in business, the top two being lack of vision and lack of character.

With vision, you can endure, because you see the end result. You see it inside you, and use faith as your evidence that it is coming to pass in the natural realm.

> **While we look not at the things which are seen, but at the things which are not seen: for the things which are seen are temporal; but the things which are not seen are eternal.**
>
> **2 Corinthians 4:18**

A study of 500 bankrupt businesses revealed three major causes:

1. Lack of vision
2. Lack of organization
3. Lack of service

HOW DO WE RECEIVE VISION?

A vision doesn't spontaneously drop from the sky. A vision must be sought, a vision must be seen, and a vision must be shared.

> **Call to Me and I will answer you and show you great and mighty things, fenced in and hidden, which you do not know (do not distinguish and recognize, have knowledge of and understand).**
>
> **Jeremiah 33:3 AMP**

> **But they that wait upon the LORD shall renew their strength; they shall mount up with wings as**

---

[4] http://www.forbes.com/sites/mikemyatt/2012/01/12/businesses-dont-fail-leaders-do/

**eagles; they shall run, and not be weary; and they
shall walk, and not faint.**

Isaiah 40:31

I was a young, inexperienced pastor with a church of 125 members. It *seemed* that the logical thing to do would have been to swing into action with programs and ministries to grow the church. Instead, I found an old musty boiler room and waited there before the Lord. Early each morning, I began seeking God there. I didn't want to be like Eli the lazy priest. After waiting, I began to feel like a bird mounting up with an aerial view; I started *seeing* a vision inside of me.

I saw this verse in a new light.

**And the next Sabbath day came almost the whole
city together to hear the word of God.**

Acts 13:44

Hope came alive in my heart! As I waited on the Lord, I began to see what faith could accomplish in our church. I was encouraged to know that there was a time in history when almost an entire city came to hear God's Word. I knew if it happened before, it could happen again. I began to see the possibilities of church growth, and that Scripture became enormously real to my heart.

Faith is the substance of things hoped for, the evidence of things not seen.

Hebrews 11:1

Without hope (a dream, a vision) faith cannot operate. Back then we only had a handful of members, but I began to envision ushers setting up chairs every week to accommodate all the people who would be coming to Christ and desiring to be true disciples. I could not be satisfied with only 125 members when

36

the city had over 80,000 people. A farmer would not be satisfied with a few stalks of corn or wheat. He wants the full harvest!

A QUESTION YOU MUST ANSWER

Stop now and answer this question honestly. Really think and pray about it before you answer.

Here's the question: **Ten years from now, where will you be, and what will you be doing?**

Vision will cause you to make your mark on this world, if you divide that vision into micro-steps and take action.

God has a vision for you. How do you see yourself? God sees you for what you can become. He gave Jesus Christ for you. If you haven't already, give your life to Jesus and he will impart vision that will lift you to great victories.

Again, I repeat: **If you are willing to see the invisible, you can accomplish the impossible.**

May I suggest that you begin a prayer-dream book? Get a notebook and start putting pictures of your preferred future, along with God's P romises and your special notes and faith declarations. You can cut out pictures from magazines or download images of things you want to be part of your future. Remember, "Faith is the substance of things hoped for...."

I started the practice of making prayer-dream books as a young preacher. I started with a notebook I purchased for ten cents at a discount store. I wrote God's promises in the book, my faith declarations, prayers, and even cut out pictures from magazines and pasted them in my prayer-dream book.

Back in those days, I had five preacher heroes. I pasted their pictures on a poster along with my own picture. Over time, all five of them became my dear friends. I've sat and enjoyed meals with men and women that millions of others would love to have just a chance to meet. I've been in their homes, prayed with them, and caught some of their anointing.

Was this all a coincidence, or was it because God saw my faith when I put together that childlike poster? You can decide for yourself. But as for me, silly as it may seem, after nearly forty years in ministry I still make prayer-dream books and posters to express my vision of the future.

In the next chapter, you will learn how to move from the vision to faith forecasting.

V1 **Values:** Stemming from God's Word

V2 **Vision:** Your General Concept, Dream, or Desire

V3 **Voicing:** Making Your Faith Forecast

V4 **Vividness:** Setting Faith Goals, Plans, Organizing

V5 **Visioning:** Seeing it in Your Inner Person in Detail

V6 **Vitalizing:** Bringing Life to Faith Goals by Action

V7 **Victory:** Seeing Your Dream Realized

CHAPTER 4

FAITH FORECASTING

The substitute Sunday school teacher was struggling to open a combination lock on a supply cabinet. She had been given the combination but forgot it. She fumbled around trying to get the door to open. She didn't want to bother the pastor but she had no choice.

She shyly went to the pastor's study and said, "Pastor I can't get the supply cabinet open because I forgot the combination." So the pastor went to the cabinet with her.

He looked at the lock and then he looked up as if he were looking up to heaven. He dialed a number on the lock and then he looked up again. Once again he dialed another number.

The substitute teacher stared in awe. *He is praying. He's getting words from heaven*, she thought. Finally the lock clicked open. Totally amazed at the pastor's faith she blurted, "Pastor, I am in awe of your faith."

The pastor responded, "Oh, it was nothing; we've got the combination on a piece of masking tape stuck on the ceiling."

He could see something that she didn't see.

SEEING WHAT OTHERS DO NOT SEE

Are you seeing what others don't see? Are you seeing the destiny God has planned for you? Can you envision the creative plan God designed for your life?

In 1980, I went to New York I met Dr. David Yonggi Cho for the first time. At that time, Dr. Cho was pastoring the largest church in the world, with 80,000 members, in Seoul, Korea. By the time he retired, his church had over 800,000 members! Working with God through faith goals, faith forecasts, and faith vision, Dr. Cho became pastor of the world's largest church in all of history.

MY LIFE WAS DRAMATICALLY IMPACTED

He spoke about making faith forecasts and seeing things that others don't see. My life was dramatically changed for the better. I began to see things that others didn't see. I began to learn how to penetrate the realm of God's Spirit and to creatively develop vision.

This is one characteristic that sets apart winners and achievers from whiners and drifters in life. It's something that will enable you to treat the future as the present, the unseen as the seen, and to call those things that are not yet as though they were.[1]

This practice I call faith *forecasting* or *voicing your vision*, can profoundly enhance your tomorrow. It's an exercise in intimacy with God, worship of God, and collaboration with God.

Question: **Are you seeing what others don't see?**

PROPHETIC REVELATION FROM GOD

Jeremiah, the prophet, understood how to see what others do not see. God gave a prophetic promise through Jeremiah. Let's read this prophetic promise in a few different translations.

---

[1] Romans 4:17

42

Call unto me, and I will answer thee, and show thee
great and mighty things, which thou knowest not.

Jeremiah 33:3 KJV

Ask me and I will tell you remarkable secrets you do
not know about things to come.

Jeremiah 33:3 NLT

Call to Me and I will answer you and show you
great and mighty things, fenced in and hidden, which
you do not know (do not distinguish and recognize,
have knowledge of and understand).

Jeremiah 33:3 AMP

2-3 "This is GOD's Message, the God who made
earth, made it livable and lasting, known everywhere
as GOD: 'Call to me and I will answer you. I'll tell you
marvelous and wondrous things that you could never
figure out on your own.'"

Jeremiah 33:2–3 MSG

God essentially promised, "If you will call on me, I'll
give you revelation that you never could have figured out
on your own."[2]

Have you ever faced a frustrating situation where you
just didn't know what to do? Here God is offering you an
answer—a solution.

Now I'd like you to do something Dr. Cho instructed me to
do back in 1980. After you read the following four questions,
I'd like you to close your eyes for just a moment and think
about how you would answer them:

- What do you see for your life two years down
  the road from today?
- How about ten years ahead? What do you see?

---

[2] You may want to listen to my audio series: *Engaging the Prophetic Realm*, Decapolis Publishing. Call 800-888-7284, or visit www.davewilliams.com to order.

- **What does your dream future look like?**
- **What do you see for your personal life, your family life, your work, your ministry, your finances, and career?**

Go ahead, close your eyes and meditate on these questions.

A FAITH FORECAST CONSIDERS ONLY GOD'S ABILITY

An authentic faith forecast doesn't take into consideration the economic situation, the political situation, or any other circumstance other than the faith situation. A faith forecast is made when you believe God's promises and, by faith, embed those promises into your life through faith declarations. I call these declarations faith forecasts—voicing your vision.

God has a passion—almost an obsession—to be believed. In fact, he declared that he only rewards those who exercise faith and seek him sincerely.

> **But without faith it is impossible to please him: for he that cometh to God must believe that he is, and that he is a rewarder of them that diligently seek him.**
>
> **Hebrews 11:6**

This may be why so many needs go unmet. This could be the reason people have dreams that go unfulfilled—they're not bringing pleasure to God by using faith.

The writer to Hebrews said it is impossible to please God without faith. Even prayers that are not prayed in faith accomplish nothing and are not pleasing to God. You can whine and cry for three or four hours and still not be rewarded. Scripture says anyone who wants to come to God *must believe*:

1. That God exists
2. That he rewards those who sincerely seek him

So, God has a passion about being believed, and God loves to reward those who will believe in him and those who will exercise faith. Faith goals, faith forecasts, and faith actions make God smile.

ARTICULATED VISION—ROOTED IN GOD'S PROMISES

What is a faith forecast? A faith forecast is an articulated vision, rooted in God's promises. You use your faith to forecast your future, based on God's covenant promises.

You have the dream or vision. Now make your faith forecast concerning it. Speak it! Announce it! Proclaim it with words. Talk to a trusted friend about it.

When I was a pastor in Lansing, I developed a plan for communication that I tried always to follow. First, I would speak with God until I had a clear picture of what he desired. For example, when God gave me the dream of a global prayer center, I talked with him until I had it clear in my mind and heart what he wanted. Next, I talked to my wife, Mary Jo. Often I would make faith forecasts to her, and she would start praying, even though some of my dreams have been almost scary to her...until God also spoke to her heart.

Then, if the dream (or vision) involved our church, I would communicate it to my staff. Next, I'd share with the official board, then the intercessors, next the lay leaders, next the members, and finally the public.

God has a passion to be believed and without a vision and an expressed faith forecast, your future will probably be much the same as it is today. It might be a little worse, it might be a little better, but for all intents and purposes your future will be just about the same. You won't have much of a future without a vision. Without a faith forecast that is expressed in words, rooted in God's Word, we have no future.

Proverbs tells us where there is no vision, the people perish. And that word *perish* means collapse, crumble, crash, disintegrate, rot, or dissolve. It's the opposite of revival, renewal, and increase. Where there is no vision, the people, the business, the church, or the ministry will collapse, crumble, crash, disintegrate, rot, or dissolve. Where there is no vision, the family will rot and eventually dissolve. Without a faith forecast—a vision that is articulated—we begin to rot. That's why I say there is no future without a faith forecast.

WHO WOULD INVEST IN A SINKING BOAT?

Many years ago a pastor from another community asked if he could have lunch with me because he wanted some counsel. So we went to lunch, and after a very short time I realized he didn't really want counsel.

He told me how terrible his church board was, how bad the church was, how badly they were paying him and he couldn't afford to raise four children on his pay. He moaned that he wanted to go to school, but the board wouldn't give him the time off. He droned on and on about how his church was shrinking. The membership decreased from one hundred and fifty down to sixty. Then it happened. He revealed the real reason he wanted to meet with me. "I was wondering," he whined, "if maybe you could infuse us with some money from your missions' budget?"

Let me ask you a question: Would you invest in a stock that's performing like that? Would you make an investment in a sinking ship? Would you invest in a farmer that plants his seeds on pavement instead of rich soil?

So I explained that we *do* help churches quite often, but when we do, I always ask to see the pastor's written vision for his church.

"What is your vision?" I gently asked.

"My what?" he asked, perplexed.

Again I repeated my question a little differently by asking, "What's your faith forecast for your church's future?"

He said, "Well, I've never really thought about it."

"Let me see if I understand you correctly," I probed. "You've been pastor for four years now and you've never thought about your vision?"

I told him that if he slipped away to a private place and focused on articulating a vision that he could *voice* to the church and community, then we would talk again about support. I wasn't surprised when I never heard from him again. He left the ministry and I don't know where he went or what he's doing now.

When a pastor or leader presents a clear, meaningful vision that can be written down in words, and makes faith forecasts based on that vision, the church begins to demonstrate harmony, stability, and growth. The same is true in any enterprise you undertake.

Confusion and dissenion are the result when a leader does not have a comprehensive vision. Boards and committees then start dictating the direction. When that happens, there will always be competing visions, and that spells "di-vision!"

WITHOUT A FAITH FORECAST, THERE IS NO FUTURE

What does God see for your future? What destiny has God laid out for you?

There is no future without a faith forecast. There is no future without a vision that is well articulated. A faith forecast is a vision articulated; it is a clear picture of an exceptional future imparted by a loving and extraordinary God. It's not about God's ability to provide an abundantly fruitful future, but about our capacity to receive it.

It's like this; the ocean doesn't care if you take water from it. The ocean doesn't care if you go down with a teaspoon or a tablespoon. It doesn't care if you go down with a coffee mug or a 55 gallon drum and fill it with water. It doesn't even matter if you take a big tanker truck, back it up to the ocean and draw a whole tanker load out. The ocean doesn't care. No matter how much you take, it doesn't deplete the ocean's supply of water.

It's the same with God. God has an inexhaustible supply. Regardless of the circumstances, regardless of the situation, he told you to open your mouth wide (ask) and he will fill it. He has an endless supply. You can boldly declare, "I possess an inexhaustible supply, thanks to my God!"[3]

We live in time. Time has three phases: past, present, future. God lives in eternity. Eternity encompasses all three of those phases. That's how God can go back and forgive our sins from twenty years ago. And that's how he can go forward and change our future. He is the "I Am." He's in the past, the present, and the future. I don't understand that completely, but I lean not on my own understanding; I just trust God.

In a faith forecast, you can go to a private place and chat with Jesus. I've always called it my "private garden."

I don't know where your private garden is; it may be in the basement, an upstairs closet, or even a real garden. This is the place where you go to call out to God because there are things you can't figure out on your own. There are things you need to know about the future that the Holy Spirit will show you.

So Jesus steps from the future and brings you a word in the present that tells you something about your future so you can take aim now using faith goals. It may be a simple prophetic word.

---

[3] Philippians 4:19; Psalm 81:10

My wife and I visited Christ for the Nations in Dallas, Texas, in 1979 for a special conference. Mary Jo had graduated from the school a few years before. There was a minister named Chuck Flynn, who spoke at this conference, who said he would prophesy over people who wanted to stay after the service. Mary Jo and I stood in line waiting. I was nervous, but when he put his hands on me he prophesied, saying my ministry was about to change. He continued, "Don't be afraid of it. When you get back home you're going to find a change in your ministry and don't be afraid of it." Then he told me of some of the struggles I'd face in the future. He said, "Don't quit. When you face these challenges, don't quit."

It wasn't too long after we arrived home that I received a phone call. My pastor called to ask if I would like to come on staff as his associate pastor. At that time, I was working more as an evangelist with a radio broadcast to five states. But everything was about to change.

I told him, "Well, ah...ah...I never wanted to be a pastor."

Just then the Holy Spirit reminded me of Reverend Flynn's words—that little prophetic fragment of revelation brought from the future about my destiny. I thought, *maybe God does want me to be a pastor for some reason unknown to me right now.* It's something I never thought I wanted, but I started thinking maybe God wanted me to take this step.

So, I became a pastor...and remained a pastor for the next thirty-one years. I faced the precise things I was warned about in the prophecy, but never once seriously thought of quitting.

A faith forecast, a vision that is articulated and rooted in God's promises, is often when Jesus steps out of the future and gives you a word or a fragment, a picture, something related to your destiny, so you can begin to make faith forecasts now.

How does it work? Faith is what pleases God, and if you want to be a God pleaser you'll want to understand faith forecasting. I've always felt that when you need a definition for something you should go to God's Word for the definition.

Don't go to *Webster's Dictionary* or *The American Standard Dictionary* for the definition of a biblical word or concept. Go to God's Word for the definition, and here is God's definition of the word *faith*.

> [1] **Now faith is the substance of things hoped for, the evidence of things not seen.**
>
> [2] **For by it the elders obtained a good report.**
>
> [3] **Through faith we understand that the worlds were framed by the word of God, so that things which are seen were not made of things which do appear.**
>
> **Hebrews 11:1–3**

If we're talking about faith forecasting, we've got to know what true faith really is. Because there is an illusionary faith that leads to nothing but daydreams, mirages and hallucinations, all of which bring no lasting fruit to our lives.

Faith is what pleases God.[4] Remember, God has a passion to be believed, an obsession to be believed, and God rewards those who believe him and diligently seek him.

Faith is substance.[5] Let's think about "substance" for a minute. What is substance? Substance is the essence; it's the center, the crux, the foundation. It is the subject matter of thought, discourse, study, etc. Substance is the actual matter of a thing, as opposed to the appearance or shadow. Substance is the reality.

The reverse of substance is deficiency, emptiness, scarcity, shortage, reduction, inadequacy. When pastors continually say things like, "In this bad economy..." and they complain about shortages and reductions, do you know what they're

---

[4] Hebrews 11:6
[5] Hebrews 11:1

doing? They are painting a picture for their congregation to see. They're making a faith forecast, only it's in reverse. It's a forecast of shortage and reduction.

That kind of talk is faithless talk. In other words, no faith, no pleasing God. Speaking of scarcity does not please God.

FAITH IS THE ESSENCE OF THINGS HOPED FOR

Faith is substance; it's the essence of what? Answer: Things! What are things? You know what things are! Things are objects or objectives. Things are specifics or goals.

What kind of things? Answer: The things you hope for. Faith is the substance—the essence—of the things you hope for. What is hope? Hope is not just some wishy-washy, unsure optimism. Hope is your picture of the future. A faith forecast puts concrete words to that picture.

I served in the U.S. Navy for four years, mostly aboard a destroyer. That's a fairly small ship. We had about 250 sailors onboard, and when we were out to sea for a long time we would run low on supplies. There wasn't enough room on that little ship to store all the supplies we needed. Whether we needed food supplies, armaments, spare parts, or whatever, an announcement would come over the loudspeakers, "Attention. A supply ship will arrive at 1600 hours. All hands report to the main deck at that time to receive supplies."

Now that announcement was kind of like a faith forecast. We knew that at 4:00 o'clock in the afternoon (1600 hours), there would be a supply ship coming alongside of our little destroyer. And what would happen? They would shoot a small rope over to our ship and someone would pull it on board. Attached to that small rope was a heavy cable. And they'd pull that heavy cable over to our ship and secure it and, sure enough, it wasn't long before we were getting 50 pounds of meat here, 100 pounds of fresh vegetables there, or a load of armaments. The supplies would just keep coming until we had everything we needed and the storage compartments were filled.

Hope is like a cable that's connected to Jesus. God has an inexhaustible supply for you. Even when you don't see it yet, a faith forecast keeps saying, "It's coming and I have it. I have it, even though I don't yet see it with my eyes."

Remember, *God has a passion to be believed.* If I believed that announcement that said we were receiving supplies at 1600 hours, why wouldn't I believe the promises of God?

When you stay attached to Jesus, you have an unlimited supply line connected to the "ship" of your life. Understanding and believing this will intensely affect your future.

Hope is what gives us vision. David had a vision of building a great temple for God. He even made the plans in writing.[6] He never was permitted to build it, but do you know what God said? "David, because it was in your heart to do it, I'm going to give you credit for it."

This means our vision and our faith forecasts should stretch way beyond our own lives. I repeat—God has a passion to be believed.

Biblical hope is never static or passive. It's dynamic, active; it's life-sustaining. In other words, when we heard that the ship was coming alongside to deliver us pancake mix and meat, somebody had to be ready to pull the cable from the supply ship to ours. We had to take some action. Even when we were pulling the cable over we still didn't have the food, but we were preparing to receive the supplies. We could not have a passive attitude: "Ys, I hope they have food coming to us from the supply ship. Oh, if they wanted us to have food it would simply appear." No, we had to do three things:

---

[6] 1 Chronicles 28:19

1. Believe the announcement
2. Prepare to receive the supplies
3. Cooperate in receiving the supplies

Do you prepare to receive from God when you pray in faith?

When you voice a faith forecast for your life, calling those things which be not as though they are, you always root it in God's Word.

In other words, we've all heard people making mindless talk. "I'm going to talk positive," they say, "And every day, in every way, I'm getting better and better." (No you're not. I knew you a year ago and you've gotten worse and worse over that year.)

These so called faith forecasts and declarations *that have no action added* become the beginning of delusion. When we refuse to add action to our faith, we are inviting a delusion. Declarations and confessions without some kind of faith action lead only to fruitless fantasies. It's like the person who says, "If God wanted to fill me with the Holy Spirit, he'd just come down and do it." No, it's a partnership. You do the natural, God does the super, and together it becomes supernatural.

God calls those things that are not yet as though they already are (Romans 4:17).

I remember walking into the pulpit and saying to our congregation, "I want you all to close your eyes." (I learned this from Dr. Cho back in 1980).

I continued, "I want you to see something. I want you to see yourself pulling into a driveway with all these colorful flags flying, representing nations of the world where we are supporting missionaries. Can you see it?"

Everybody excitedly hollered, "Yeah, yeah, we can see it!"

Then I directed, "Now I want you to see yourself walking into a brand new worship center with three thousand seats all filled with worshippers of Jesus."

You could actually hear people trying to catch their breath. After all, at that time we were only a congregation of 400 or so. Faith and excitement filled the hearts and minds of the congregation. They could *see* it.

Afterward a deacon came and put his arm around my shoulder and warned, "Look, Brother Williams, you don't want to be getting these people's hopes up like that. We'll probably only need about 1,200 seats."

But I wouldn't compromise the vision by making a watered down faith forecast of only needing 1,200 seats. It was a good thing, too!

In 1987, on the opening day of our new 3,000 seat worship center, over 2,800 people were already attending. And the deacon who warned me not to make such a bold faith forecast was gone.

Don't ever compromise your faith forecast. People will try to get you to compromise it. Don't do it. Don't miss your destiny because of somebody else's lack of faith or human reasoning. You may be required to change the route, but never take an exit from the vision born in your heart by the Holy Spirit.

Views of Mount Hope Church in Lansing, Michigan.

Make your faith forecast based on your values and your vision and keep forecasting even if everything looks dismal. The more you voice your faith forecasts, the clearer your vision will come into focus. And that's what we will discover next: how to bring vividness to your vision.

Main entrance to Mount Hope Church featuring flags of just some of the countries supported by the church's missions giving.

V1 **Values:** Stemming from God's Word

V2 **Vision:** Your General Concept, Dream, or Desire

V3 **Voicing:** Making Your Faith Forecast

V4 **Vividness:** Setting Faith Goals, Plans, Organizing

V5 **Visioning:** Seeing it in Your Inner Person in Detail

V6 **Vitalizing:** Bringing Life to Faith Goals by Action

V7 **Victory:** Seeing Your Dream Realized

CHAPTER

BRINGING VIVIDNESS TO YOUR VISION

When the Lord gave me the dream for our 3000 seat worship center in Lansing, I didn't know exactly how it would happen. I had never managed a construction project in my life. I was the butt of jokes, sarcasm, and insults for a couple of years because my dream was "too big" for our little town. But the Lord helped me to set micro-steps toward the achievement of this macro-picture. God, working with me and my team, brought the project to completion. Yes, there were setbacks, challenges, and obstacles to overcome, but when the dream became a reality, over 2800 worshippers were already in attendance on the opening day.

> ^{25} **Look straight ahead and fix your eyes on what lies before you.**
>
> ^{26} **Mark out a straight path for your feet; stay on the safe path.**
>
> **Proverbs 4:25–26 (NLT)**

If today you conducted a survey on the street asking people about their specific goals, only a few would be able to tell you in direct, concise terms what their goals in life are. The other ninety-five percent would have no goals at all or only general dreams such as "to be happy" or "to be healthy." Those are not goals, and they certainly aren't faith goals, but only nonspecific wishes. They are great wishes, but without faith goals—specific steps to reach them—they remain only stargazing wishes with no power to come true.

WHY GOALS ARE IMPORTANT

A goal is a target—a specific aim. How can you hit a target if you don't know where it is? You'll be shooting all over, but probably never hitting anything except the things that just happen to be in the way. This is a gross waste of time and energy.

I am so grateful that someone introduced me to U.S. Congressman Ed Foreman back in the early years of my ministry. He, in a fun way, taught me the value of having clear goals. Later I was introduced to America's foremost business philosopher, Jim Rohn, who conducted a special seminar to teach his students how to set goals. Jim asked his students to share these concepts with business groups, Sunday Schools, and grandchildren. I am grateful for these two early mentors in my life. I needed to understand goal setting before I could come to grips with the concept of establishing faith goals.

GOALS HELP YOU SIMPLIFY AND MOVE FORWARD

When I was a young boy growing up in Jackson, Michigan, my brother and I would go to the park and play on the merry-go-round. We'd push it as we ran around in a circle to get it going, then hop on and whirl around and around. We spun so fast we got dizzy. But we weren't getting anywhere! Though we were moving, and moving fast, we were only spinning around in circles. That's what happens when you have no specific goals. You may be moving, and moving fast, but one day you'll realize that you haven't really gotten anywhere—there has been no significant progress.

Every sport has goals. Think about it. In basketball, the hoop is the goal. In football, it's a touchdown. Hockey, base-ball...any sport has a "goal." Without goals we never know for sure if we are scoring or making significant progress.

Having no goals—concrete goals—is like trying to oper-ate an ocean liner without a helmsman. You set out to sea, just hoping to drift to the right port. Your chances are about one in 999 trillion (in other words, zero) that you'll end up where you want to go! The same is true when you don't have specific goals. You drift through life, hoping to arrive somewhere, only to tragically discover that you've drifted around and around, reaching nowhere, and achieving nothing of real significance.

Picture yourself going to the airport to buy a ticket. You walk up to the counter and say, "I'd like a ticket, please."

"What is your destination, sir?" the ticket agent asks.

"Oh, I don't know. Anywhere, I guess. Just give me a ticket."

That sounds foolish, doesn't it? But how many individuals try to gain success in life without even knowing where they want to go and without setting clear-cut goals for getting there?

Some of the construction volunteers from our church planned to travel to Honduras to build a Bible School. They had goals—specific goals. The general dream was: **"Build a Bible School in Honduras."** Now, the specific goals were:

- **Drive to Detroit (date, time, location etc.)**
- **Fly from Detroit to Miami (airline, time, date)**
- **Fly from Miami to Honduras (airline, time, date)**

- Arrive in Honduras; check into hotel for night (date, time, hotel)
- Start work (date, time, location)

Now please notice that some goals are just common sense. That's why I call them "goals" instead of "faith goals." I don't need a faith goal to figure out which way I should drive to work every day. I don't need a faith goal to determine which flight to take to Atlanta for a conference. Some things are merely simple, everyday goals. But when you are planning a dream much bigger than yourself, you need to set *faith* goals.

In building the Bible school, there were definite construction goals, material goals, and deadlines to meet once the team started work each morning. The team leader carefully planned everything. Planning and organizing was essential for the success of the ten-day trip. They had to accomplish what they set out to do.

WORKING BY A PLAN

God himself has always worked by plans. He has a plan for salvation, a plan for peace and joy, a plan for each individual's life. He even has a blueprint for the universe, the earth, and the oceans.

> [27] I was there when he established the heavens, when he drew the horizon on the oceans.
>
> [28] I was there when he set the clouds above, when he established springs deep in the earth.
>
> [29] I was there when he set the limits of the seas, so they would not spread beyond their boundaries. And when he marked off the earth's foundations,
>
> [30] I was the architect at his side.
>
> **Proverbs 8:27–30a NLT**

Planning is a vital stage to any project. If you fail to make plans, you'll quickly discover that circumstances, situations, problems, and other people will begin to determine your priorities. This will leave you frustrated at the end of the day, with a feeling that you've made no real accomplishments.

Author and management consultant Louis A. Allen stated, "The greatest source of long-term failure for organized endeavors undoubtedly is the failure to plan."

Careful planning puts you ahead in the long run; hurry and scurry puts you further behind.

Proverbs 21:5 MSG

Do your planning and prepare your fields before building your house.

Proverbs 24:27 NLT

If you are looking for failure, then simply neglect to make solid plans. Failure to make well thought-out plans will ensure an unsuccessful project. The downfall of ninety-eight percent of all projects that fail is the lack of proper planning.

You wouldn't consider building a house without a blueprint. Why start a project without a plan? Why try to make your God-given dreams come true without a plan for achieving them?

If you were building a huge building; you would need a plan. The builders know it would be sheer folly to attempt construction on such a great structure without a blueprint and plan of construction. Studies undeniably show that the more time you spend in advance planning for a project, the less total time is required to bring it to completion.

One of the most productive things you can do with your time is to use it to prayerfully plan. Plan your day, plan your week, plan your years, plan your business, plan your ministry, plan to see your dreams come true...counting on God to direct you.

HOW TO PLAN

How do you plan when you're counting on God to direct? Following is a simple guide to the necessary stages in the planning process. You will notice the steps are applicable to the planning of *any* task or enterprise.

1. Define Your Dream

You must first know what you want before you can plan for it. What is your dream? Write it out on a piece of paper. If you can't write out your God-given dream on a sheet of paper, then you can't plan for it. Write your dream down, read it aloud, study it, meditate upon it, and ask for God's guidance. Don't try to understand every detail about it in this first stage. This is where faith applies. Simply trust God to direct you. The important thing is that you *know what your dream is*.

Again, remember that the number one reason people don't get what they want is because they don't know what they want. One of my life's dreams is to lead people into a deeper, more fruitful fellowship with the Lord Jesus Christ, and to inspire them to use their faith in reaching their greatest potential for God. There you have it. That dream is defined. Once you can define your dream and get it on paper, God will begin to give you some ideas and steps to take for making your dream come true. Now, we will spend a considerable amount of time on the subject of faith goals because they are so important to the planning process.

2. Set a Faith Goal

There is a distinct difference between a *dream* and a *faith goal*. It's important to know the difference. Let me define both terms more clearly.

Dream (or Vision): Is an overall vision that can be pursued for indefinite amounts of time. When you invest time with the

Lord in prayer, he will place a dream on your heart, or a vision of his purposes for your life, career, ministry, or business. As you wait before the Lord, you'll find yourself "mounting up with wings as eagles," gaining an aerial view of the vision God is calling you to pursue.[1]

Faith Goal: Is a target for you to aim at within your planning period that will move you closer to realizing your God-given dream or vision.

A DREAM IS NONSPECIFIC

When I had the dream of building a world-class healing center, it was a general idea or concept. During a time of seeking the Lord, I had a vision of a kinder, gentler, healing center. It would consist of a spiritual side, with biblical counseling and support groups, and also a medical side. The medical side would have Medical and Osteopathic Physicians, Chiropractors, Naturopaths, and Homeopaths. All of these professionals would work together with God and consult with each other for the best possible plan for treating patients facing physical problems.

That's all I knew. So I articulated the concept the best I could in both spoken words and written concepts. But I didn't know how to do it. So I waited on the Lord for further instructions before I started laying out specific micro-steps toward that macro-picture. Now, this is important:

- **The dream is the "what."**
- **The faith goals are the "how."**

When you commit to the "what," God will show you the "how."

I committed myself to building Gilead Healing Center. It wasn't until nearly twenty years later the Lord spoke to my heart and said, "Now is the time!"

---

[1] Isaiah 40:40–41

"Lord, show me how," I pleaded. I knew it would take several million dollars that I didn't have. I was committed to remaining debt-free, so I told everyone we were going to build a new kind of healing center without debt. I didn't know "how," but I was committed to the "what." Day-by-day,

Scenes from Gilead Healing Center
306 S. Creyts Road, Lansing, MI 48917
www.gileadhealingcenter.com 517-319-5808

during my morning times of prayer and Bible reading, the Lord faithfully showed me the plan, revealing the people who would help, the right steps to take, and the faith goals necessary to see it to completion.

We did build it debt-free!

As an added blessing from the Lord, a regional network of medical clinics was closing in Michigan, so they donated over $4 million worth of medical equipment for the medical side of Gilead. Today there are thousands of testimonies of God's healing love that come from that "dream" that became a reality through faith goals.

A FAITH GOAL IS SPECIFIC

Faith can only go after something specific. Faith never runs after nebulous, ambiguous, unfocused, misty, and unclear thoughts! Faith is the substance of things hoped for. What do you hope for? If you have a clear vision of what you want, you can convert that vision into reality using faith goals.

The process of converting your vision, or your dream, into reality is by setting micro-steps or faith goals toward achieving the macro-picture. When I learned this, it made a monumental difference to everything—and I mean everything—in my life. Suddenly, my dreams became powerful targets that I was able to accomplish with God's help.

Setting faith goals really is the practice of intimacy with God. We don't work *for* God; we work *with* God when our goals come from him.

God has always wanted to work with us and through us. Once we understand the difference between mere goals and faith goals, we'll never overwork, get over-stressed, and certainly never burn out. We'll learn to operate *with* God instead of *for* God.

¹⁹ **So then after the Lord had spoken unto them, he was received up into heaven, and sat on the right hand of God.**

²⁰ **And they went forth, and preached everywhere, the Lord working with them, and confirming the word with signs following. Amen.**

Mark 16:19–20

The Lord was working with them, confirming his word with signs following. *The New Living Translation* says that God was working *through* them. God will work *with* you and *through* you if you'll sit down and design faith goals—micro-steps—that will daily carry you closer to your vision.

Some people's lives are like treadmills, some are like elevators, some are like drifting leaves. However, some people's lives are like guided missiles. Faith goal setters are guided missiles. They shoot for a target and receive guidance along the way.

Think of it. A survey showed seventy-four percent of people say they feel their life is on a treadmill. They never dare to do what's important to them. One consulting firm, with an impressive list of clients, discovered that ninety-nine percent of the people they surveyed felt they were capable of accomplishing more, but they weren't. Do you believe you could accomplish a whole lot more than you've accomplished up to this point?

The top three reasons identified for not reaching goals were:

1. Procrastination

2. Lack of discipline

3. No game plan

Ninety-five percent of the people in the world do not have any kind of goals, and thus they fall into what psychologists call the "underachiever" category. Five percent of the people in the world possess goals. Those in the five percent achieve more than the ninety-five percent combined who have no established goals. That shows you the power of goals.

And I'm going to show you the even greater power of setting *faith* goals. A goal is a checkpoint on your journey through life. It is a specific target to reach within a period of time along the way to making your God-given dreams come true.

If you don't learn to set clear-cut goals, you will probably never rise above mediocrity. With no goals, your life will just drift with the circumstances. And this is one of the greatest causes of failure—just drifting with the tide. St. Paul said,

> **So I run with purpose in every step. I am not just shadowboxing.**
>
> **1 Corinthians 9:26 NLT**

> **I press on toward the goal to win the [supreme and heavenly] prize to which God in Christ Jesus is calling us upward.**
>
> **Philippians 3:14 AMP**

Why do people get addicted to drugs and alcohol?
Why do people become ensnared by false cults?
Why do tens of thousands get in trouble with the law?
Why are so many people struggling financially?
Why are so many struggling with relationships?

In many cases the answer is quite simple: These people have no plans, no goals, and no definitive purpose in life. They are like the man the Beatles sang about years ago....

> He's a real nowhere Man,
> Sitting in his Nowhere Land,
> Making all his nowhere plans,
> For nobody.
>
> Doesn't have a point of view,
> Knows not where he's going to,
> Isn't he a bit like you and me?[2]

---

[2] Lennon, John; McCartney, Paul; *Nowhere Man*, © Sony/ATV Music Publishing LLC, Universal Music Publishing Group.

What about you?

- **Do you know who you are in Christ?**
- **Do you know God's direction for your life?**
- **Do you know where you are going in this life?**
- **Do you know where you are going after this life is over?**
- **Do you have specific faith goals for your life right now?**

Sigmund Freud, the Austrian founder of psychoanalysis, said that goals are dangerous because there is a chance of failing to reach them. Then, if failure occurs, your self-respect will be damaged and you will become neurotic. Isn't that something?

It's interesting to note that he didn't practice what he preached. Freud himself had goals. He had aspirations. He wrote books and reports and had goals that would help him propagate his strange, new ideas back in the late 1800 and early 1900 hundreds. Freud was wrong.

The failure to set a goal is—*by far*—worse than not reaching it. For example, it is much better for a student to set his goal for an "A" average and get a "B" average, than to set no goal and get a "D" average. Failure to set goals is tragic.

I have a goal to read 52 books each year. But suppose my schedule gets hectic, I miss my goal, and only read 38 books in a year? Have I failed? I still read 38 books, thereby improving my education, helping my career, and creating a better future for my family.

IN WHAT AREAS SHOULD YOU SET FAITH GOALS?

I believe that every human being should sit down and prayerfully set specific faith goals in each important area of life. You may set faith goals for:

- **Your spiritual life**
- **Your health and fitness**
- **Your marriage and family life**
- **Your education**
- **Your career**
- **Your ministry or charitable involvement**
- **Your finances and investments**
- **Your "things" (any things you want to have)**

> **Therefore I say unto you, What things soever ye desire, when ye pray, believe that ye receive them, and ye shall have them.**
>
> **Mark 11:24**

Satan will probably work hard to keep you from setting faith goals and getting organized. This is because he knows the value of the practice. He will seek to convince you to put it off until a more convenient time. Or he will tell you that it's too much trouble to set faith goals and make plans. Sometimes he persuades people with the lie that they don't have what it takes to enjoy a remarkable life of great achievement and contentment.

Why not schedule a ten to twelve hour block of time right now? Take that time to sit down alone and prayerfully plan your future. Ask the Holy Spirit to be involved with you in getting a vision—a dream—and setting some specific faith targets toward reaching that dream. It will dramatically change you, advance you, and will be the beginning of your leap to greater achievement.

THE MIRACLE OF MAKING LISTS

Creating your faith goals necessitates list making.

Successful people are almost always list-makers. List making may seem pointless to you in the beginning, but investing some time into this simple practice can infuse miraculous results into your life. The Bible says:

"Call unto me...."[3]

"Ask and it shall be given...."[4]

"You have not because you ask not...."[5]

God, it seems, is screaming for his children to make him a list. What do you want? What faith goal do you desire God to help you with? Where's your list?

In my **Pastor's School**, I ask the students to list fifty things they really want in life, home, work, achievements, and other things—anything! Sadly, less than eleven percent can list fifty things they really want.

People make lists in their own style. Each of us is different and unique. You may not follow my plan exactly, but the important thing is that you list your faith goals in a way that works for you.

Richard Branson, founder of the Virgin Group, wrote this in his blog: "I have always lived my life by making lists. These vary from lists of people to call, lists of ideas, lists of companies to set up, lists of people who can make things happen. I also have lists of topics to blog about, lists of tweets to send, and lists of upcoming plans. Each day I work through these lists, and it is by ticking off each task that my ideas take shape and plans move forward."[6]

In 1726, at the age of 20, Benjamin Franklin created a list of goals to assist in developing his character. In his autobiography, [7] Franklin listed his thirteen "virtue goals" as:

---

[3] Jeremiah 33:3

[4] Matthew 7:7; Luke 11:9

[5] James 4:2; John 16:24

[6] www.virgin.com/richard-branson/blog/top-10-tips-for-making-lists

[7] Franklin, Benjamin, *The Autobiography of Benjamin Franklin (1791)*, Dover Publications, Minneola, NY, 1996.

1. **Temperance.** Eat not to dullness; drink not to elevation.
2. **Silence.** Speak not but what may benefit others or yourself; avoid trifling conversation.
3. **Order.** Let all your things have their places; let each part of your business have its time.
4. **Resolution.** Resolve to perform what you ought; perform without fail what you resolve.
5. **Frugality.** Make no expense but to do good to others or yourself; i.e., waste nothing.
6. **Industry.** Lose no time; be always employed in something useful; cut off all unnecessary actions.
7. **Sincerity.** Use no hurtful deceit; think innocently and justly, and, if you speak, speak accordingly.
8. **Justice.** Wrong none by doing injuries, or omitting the benefits that are your duty.
9. **Moderation.** Avoid extremes; forbear resenting injuries so much as you think they deserve.
10. **Cleanliness.** Tolerate no uncleanness in body, clothes, or habitation.
11. **Tranquility.** Be not disturbed at trifles, or at accidents common or unavoidable.
12. **Chastity.** Rarely use venery but for health or offspring, never to dullness, weakness, or the injury of your own or another's peace or reputation.
13. **Humility.** Imitate Jesus and Socrates.

When you, like Benjamin Franklin, wholeheartedly determine to get your faith goals on paper, you will automatically increase your chances of hitting the target. The best insurance for hitting the bull's eye is to aim toward a specific target—a goal. Do it today!

Where's your list?[8]

V1 Values: Stemming from God's Word

V2 Vision: Your General Concept, Dream, or Desire

V3 Voicing: Making Your Faith Forecast

V4 Vividness: Setting Faith Goals, Plans, Organizing

V5 Visioning: Seeing it in Your Inner Person in Detail

V6 Vitalizing: Bringing Life to Faith Goals by Action

V7 Victory: Seeing Your Dream Realized

CHAPTER

WHERE'S YOUR LIST?

This would be a great time to start your dream list. When you begin to list the "things" spoken of in Mark 11:24 and Hebrews 11:1–3, remember money is no object. Faith will be all the substance you need. God gives you the desires of your heart, and if you list something out of harmony with his will, God can change your desires.

> **Delight thyself also in the Lord: and he shall give thee the desires of thine heart.**
>
> **Psalm 37:4**

Many years ago, I wanted a certain kind of car. I had the color picked out, the model, everything. But as I prayed and dreamed about it, my desire changed to a different make and model. Good thing! The one I was originally dreaming about turned out to be a lemon of a car that was taken off the market. And the car I ended up getting was perfect for my family and just kept going and going and was great on gas. God knew the other car would be pulled from the market and changed my desire. He always gives guidance on the go. Remember, God lives in the future, just as he lives in the present.

Vision and faith goals will trump money, talent, and brains every time. So, when making your list, don't even consider money, talent, intelligence, background, or anything except faith.

When you make a list in faith, you'll never have to kick the proverbial doors down in order to succeed. Your senior partner, Jesus, will be opening all the necessary doors.[1] You will never pressure other people to "get onboard" with your dream. God will move on the right hearts to help you and guide you.

COMPETENCY LEVELS

You probably know what business schools teach about competence and incompetence. I'll explain in a moment. But first I want you to know that in the beginning, you'll probably not be too competent at articulating a dream or vision, setting faith goals, or even making a list of things you want. But the more you practice the V7 Strategy for achieving your faith goals, the more competent you will become, until you finally get to a point where you actually do it unconsciously.

Many business courses teach us the four levels of competency. Let's apply them to setting and reaching our faith goals.

Level 1—The unconscious incompetent

This is usually the clueless "know-it-all." He doesn't need to read a book or attend a seminar. He never needs a mentor because he's so brilliant in his own mind. He's a macho man. She's a wonder woman. Neither needs anyone else to impart into his or her life. They make excuses for not learning: "Costs too much," "I don't believe they should charge for a seminar," "Oh, it's the same old stuff—I know all that." The Bible has a name for the unconscious incompetent—"fool!"

---

1 Revelation 3:7–8

Level 2—The conscious incompetent.

This is a wonderful place to be—realizing you don't know how to do something in a proficient way. You become conscious of your incompetency in a certain area. If you know you are not well trained in articulating a vision or writing out your faith goals, then, praise the Lord! You are a teachable candidate for becoming competent in these practices. You have taken the first step by reading this far. Good for you and congratulations!

Level 3—The conscious competent.

This is the magnificent level where you have achieved proficiency at setting and reaching your faith goals, but it still requires major focus and attention. You have become savvy at list making, faith goal setting, achieving things of importance, yet you find it still requires a great deal of concentration and work. I believe this is a great level that, with lots of practice, leads to the fourth level.

Level 4—The unconscious competent.

When you've reached this level, you skillfully do the things necessary for peak achievement and high-level productivity, but you do it without realizing you are doing it. You will make lists, set faith goals, reach dreams, be a high achiever and do it all at an unconscious level, barely realizing you're actually following the V7 Strategy. It's like the Word becoming flesh. The principles, concepts and actions are now a part of your life.

You are probably functioning at Level 2 or 3 right now...or you wouldn't be reading this book. So let's get some practice in list making and dreaming. Please remember what I said earlier in this chapter: Vision and faith goals will trump money, talent, and brains every time. When making your list, therefore, do not consider money, your talent, your intelligence, your education, your background, or anything else except faith.

WHAT DO YOU WANT?

Let's begin with just 15 things you want. List fifteen things you dream about. If you're dreaming about them, there's a good chance God put those dreams on your heart. Let me give you some examples of things others have listed in this exercise in my Faith Goals Seminar:

- Get a master's degree
- Take a luxury vacation (describe it)
- Have your own vacation home (where? Smoky Mountains? Palm Desert? At a nearby lake?)
- Write a book (about what? Who are your market readers?)
- Become a chef
- Get your dream car (what model? Mercedes? BMW? Cadillac? Bentley? Jaguar? Audi?)
- Pastor a unique, growing church of disciples committed to Jesus Christ (describe it)
- Give $100,000 a year to charity
- Have net assets of $10,000,000
- Get into perfect shape and fitness
- Travel (where? Europe? Greece? Holy Land? Australia? Caribbean?)
- Make a garden...or an entire farm
- Develop the greatest marriage possible
- Live in a mansion (describe it)
- Establish a wardrobe of fine clothing
- Take a missions trip (where? Medical missions? Church planting? Evangelism?)
- Open an orphanage

- Open a women's center
- Remodel my home completely (or a specific area)
- Get my law degree
- Learn a new language (Spanish? French? Russian? Portuguese?)
- Learn to play a musical instrument
- Take voice lessons
- Start a rescue mission
- Become a Big Brother or Big Sister
- Volunteer in the community hospital
- Get on the school board or city council
- Run for mayor, governor, or congress person
- Take a 12-day Caribbean cruise
- Have the lavish means to meet random needs in people's lives
- Be able to leave a waitress a $200 tip for a $29 meal if Holy Spirit reveals her urgent needs
- Own and operate a hotel, motel, or apartment building
- Read 52 books each year
- Develop a seminar on something at which you are an expert (What is it?)
- Open a specialized deli
- Start a sports team (What sport?)
- Give your parents an outrageous 50th anniversary party
- Open a neighborhood place for kids to hang out in a healthy atmosphere
- Buy a TV or radio station or whole network

- Start a podcast
- Establish a charter school
- Begin a newspaper (Print? Online?)
- Open a bank
- Own a chain of coffee shops
- Work on developing your invention. During our Club 52 intensive events, millionaire mentor and inventor, Dr. Scott Benjamin, leads the session in how to get your invention to the market. Check out www.Club52.com.
- Open a quilting shop with a weekly Bible study
- Develop an unusual series of Bible teaching
- Treat yourself and your family to an annual vacation together
- Bless your family with random surprises
- Become involved at your local school
- Develop a ministry of helps to the elderly by helping them with chores, etc.
- Be a great servant for your pastor and church
- Have no financial stress ever again!

Here's a great, true-life example of the payoff that came to one man who had faith goals and knew what he wanted. Lee Braxton had only a grade school education and couldn't even get a job as a teller at a bank. So, he started his own bank and became so successful he retired at the age of 44. Then he went on to assist full-time for a nationally known evangelist for the rest of his life. Look at this list of everything this godly man achieved—God working with him—even though he hadn't acquired a proper education:

- Served as Mayor of Whiteville, North Carolina
- Chairman of the Board, First National Bank
- President of Braxton Enterprises
- Vice-President of radio station WENC
- President, Citizens Auto Finance Company
- Owner, Columbus Finance Company
- Vice-President, Braxton-Warren Company
- President, Braxton Motor Sales, Inc.
- President, Braxton Auto Parts, Inc.
- Chairman, Public Library Board
- Chairman, Columbus County Development Committee
- Member of the Legislative Committee, North Carolina League of Municipalities
- Member of the Executive Committee, 279th District Rotary International
- National Director of Oral Roberts Global Radio and Television Broadcast
- Director, Whiteville Merchants Association and Chamber of Commerce
- Director, North Carolina Merchants Association

If Lee Braxton achieved all this without a "proper" education, think of what you can do!

Remember—*"Vision and faith goals will trump money, talent, and brains every time."*

YOU DESIRE AN EXCEPTIONAL FUTURE

I know you desire an exceptional future. Well, it starts now. You are going to become an unconscious competent in

81

dreaming and setting faith goals for your future. The more you practice, the better you will become.

Again, this is a practice in intimacy with God. When you have the faith to make your list, God will go to work with you. He will correct you along the way, help you around the detours, pole vault you over the roadblocks, and do what only he can do! God will open the right doors at the right time, and bring the right people to you at exactly the right moment. [2]

A few years ago, I listed a dream car I always wanted but felt I should not drive when I was a pastor. I told nobody about it. I built it online and copied pictures of it for my prayer/ dream book. I selected the color, the interior—everything! I planned to buy it when I retired from the pastorate and began the ministry in which I'm now involved. My main focus now is ministry to leaders in both the ministry and the marketplace.

Then something wonderful happened. At my pastoral retirement banquet, a gift awaited me from all my friends at the church. When I pulled the black cloth from the gift, it was the exact car, exact color, exact interior and exact model I had put in my prayer-dream book. Remember, I never showed any-body or told anybody about my dream car. But God knew and blessed me with the brand new, luxury car of my dreams. God will work with you when you work with him.

Now, before we go to the next chapter, write fifteen things you really want. Don't consider money, education, talent, or intelligence. Consider only this: Faith is the substance of the things you hope for and the evidence of the things you don't yet see. Are you ready? First, let's pray,

Lord, help me list things I've dreamed about
and the things you've put on my heart. Forgive me

---

2 Acts 5:19; Acts 16:26; Revelation 3:7

for limiting you in the past. I ask you to be my
partner in achieving great things in your kingdom.
Amen

Now...do it!

15 OBJECTS OR OBJECTIVES I WANT FOR MY LIFE

1. _____
2. _____
3. _____
4. _____
5. _____
6. _____
7. _____
8. _____
9. _____
10. _____
11. _____
12. _____
13. _____
14. _____
15. _____

V1 **Values:** Stemming from God's Word

V2 **Vision:** Your General Concept, Dream, or Desire

V3 **Voicing:** Making Your Faith Forecast

V4 **Vividness:** Setting Faith Goals, Plans, Organizing

V5 **Visioning:** Seeing it in Your Inner Person in Detail

V6 **Vitalizing:** Bringing Life to Faith Goals by Action

V7 **Victory:** Seeing Your Dream Realized

CHAPTER 7

GUIDELINES FOR SETTING FAITH GOALS

Now, let me offer you some helpful ideas for setting faith goals. These tips are very simple, but even though they are elementary, they will absolutely change the next twenty years of your life. If you will apply these simple guidelines you'll likely see a dramatic advance in the important areas of your life. If you haven't already, I hope you will be able to attend one of my **Faith Goals Seminars**. There I explain some remarkable, in-depth practices that will add to your skill in setting faith goals.

RULES FOR SETTING FAITH GOALS

Here are some fundamental rules for goal setting.

1. A faith goal must be specific.

Remember, faith goals—true faith goals—are not vague generalities. They are specific. They are concrete. For example, "to be used of God," is not a genuine goal; it is a vague dream. We all desire to be used of God if we are authentic Christians.

If all you have now is a vague dream, you'll want to take some time to seek the Lord in prayer to learn what is on his heart. When you discover your general calling in life, or your dream, it is easier for you to prayerfully set precise faith goals within that calling or general dream.

For instance, I am a teacher in the Body of Christ. That is the general call on my life. However, within that framework I set specific goals for teaching lessons, sermons, seminars, conferences, magazine articles, pamphlets, books, and other personal ministries. My calling is not to write a particular book. That is one of the specific faith goals *within* my calling, or *within* my God-given dream. This book, *The Miracle of Faith Goals*, for example, is the result of one faith goal within the framework of my greater vision. It's a micro-step in the macro-picture.

True goals must be specific. God created us as goal-seeking creatures, and we find it almost impossible to go after a formless, obscure, ambiguous target. But it is relatively easy for us to move toward a definite, predetermined, visualized goal. That's why faith goals, to be effective, must be explicit and concrete.

2. You should prayerfully set your own faith goals.

Of course, if you are under another's supervision, your goals will have to be set within the framework of the goals established by the leadership. Or if you work for a large company, your professional goals should be determined within the general structure of the company's corporate goals. But generally speaking, you should be the one to set your long and short-range faith goals in life. It's perfectly okay to have someone help you in the goal-setting procedure, but don't let them dictate to you what your specific aims will be.

A businesswoman once told me that her wise boss helped her set some job-related goals. He didn't actually do it for her, because he understood the importance of her actually doing it herself; he only helped her. Since setting those goals, she has advanced from sixth place to second place in sales.

The subject of goal setting is a serious matter. It could mean the difference between winning and losing, success and failure. Set your own goals after praying for God's guidance. Don't let someone else do it for you or you will lose your enthusiasm.

3. A faith goal should always take you closer to fulfilling your dream.

It's foolish to set a goal to "get a degree in chemistry" if you never plan to use chemistry in your life calling. Faith goals should always move you closer to realizing your God-given dream. If they don't, you are wasting your time. Effective, productive-minded people have learned to quit squandering time and effort in areas to which they are not called, and in which they are less than likely to succeed. Make sure your goals keep you progressing toward the fulfillment of your overall calling or vision.

For example, I was called as a pastor for over thirty years. It would have been senseless for me to set as my annual reading goal to read fifty-two unrelated books or novels. That would have helped neither me, my ministry, nor the people to whom I ministered. It would not have fit in with my God-given call, my God-given dream. So, when setting personal goals (such as reading goals) I set them with the purpose of bringing me closer to making my God-given dream come true. I always select reading materials that will help me realize the overall vision God has given me for my life and ministry.

Many ministers and professional people do not realize the consequence of violating this principle; that's why they go *backward* and not forward.

> But they hearkened not, nor inclined their ear, but
> walked in the counsels and in the imagination of their
> evil heart, and went backward, and not forward.
>
> Jeremiah 7:24

When setting your faith goals be certain they will take you closer to accomplishing your overall purpose in life. Make sure they help bring about the realization of your God-given dream.

4. A faith goal should be written down.

> ...*Write* ***the vision***, and make it plain upon tables
> Habakkuk 2:2 [italics added]

> All this, said David, the LORD made me
> understand *in writing* by his hand upon me, even all
> the works of this pattern.
> 1 Chronicles 28:19 [italics added]

These are the words of King David. Notice the valuable lessons that can be learned from this verse of Scripture:

- **The Lord was guiding David.** You also will need the guidance of the Lord in making your dreams come true.

- **David understood the plan.** It has been proven that if you can write something down on paper, you have a pretty good understanding of it.

- **He wrote out the plans, or the goals.** If you don't understand your dreams, putting them on paper in specific terms will help you gain the necessary understanding. By writing down your goal, or your idea, or your plan, it will help crystallize your thinking—something that is of paramount importance.

- **The plan was detailed; it was specific.**

Out of the five percent of people who have goals, only about three percent bother to write them down. This is true of business people, sales people, ministers, teachers, and other professional, skilled, and non-skilled people. Yet statistics prove, beyond question, that the three percent who have **written down their goals accomplish from a hundred to a thousand times more** during their lifetimes than those who have goals but never bother to write them down.

Moses prayed that God would make his people a thousand times more! And I pray that you, my friend, will be multiplied by God a thousand times as you practice setting and reaching your faith goals!

> **The Lord God of your fathers make you a thousand times so many more as ye are, and bless you, as he hath promised you!**
>
> Deuteronomy 1:11

MEASURING PROGRESS

When I was just a boy, my mom would stand me up straight against a wall on the back porch. She'd take a pencil and make a mark on the wall at the very top of my head, and write the date beside the pencil mark. Every few months she'd repeat the process to check the progress of my growth. She did the same thing with my younger brother. It was exciting to discover we had grown another inch.

That's what faith goals do for us. They provide a means of measuring progress. It's like the highway signs that tell you how much farther it is to your destination. If you were driving from Detroit to New York, and you saw a sign that read "Chicago 50 miles," you would immediately realize you were not making progress but were actually going the wrong way. You got messed up in your directions somewhere. You need to turn around. That's what faith goals do for us—they act as signposts on the journey to making your God-given dreams come true.

Goal setters will achieve more in life than those who set no goals, but sometimes the price is higher than they expected.

Faith goal setters, however, will achieve more in life than those who just drift along, and will accomplish everything with less effort because God is working with them.

> **The blessing of the Lord—it makes [truly] rich, and He adds no sorrow with it [neither does toiling increase it].**
>
> **Proverbs 10:22 AMP**

I hope you see the value of getting your goals on paper, just like that pencil mark that my mom made on the back porch showing my growth progress. When you put your goals in writing, you are not just thinking about them or talking about them, you are actually *seeing* them, producing *faith movies*. We'll discuss this further in the next chapter. Suffice it to say, *write your faith goals on paper* and you will most likely achieve a hundred to a thousand times more in your lifetime!

5. Your faith goals should be challenging, requiring faith to achieve.

A challenge creates enthusiasm, a much-needed ingredient for effective success. If you are an insurance salesman, and last year you sold 375 policies, it would be no challenge for you to set a goal this year to sell 200 policies. You already know you can do that. This goal generates no excitement or enthusiasm. But if you challenge yourself to sell 500 policies, that is an exciting, enthusiasm-producing commitment that will get results.

If a minister knows he can minister effectively to one hundred people, why should he be content to settle for that? Why shouldn't he get a God-kind of vision and set a bigger goal each year? Can you imagine Jesus saying, "I'll be satisfied if I can just get a hundred people saved and teach them the principles of the Kingdom?" Certainly not! Jesus challenged us to reach the entire world—**every single human life!** It disturbs me to hear church leaders say, "I'll be satisfied when our congregation grows to two-hundred and fifty." Well, Jesus isn't satisfied with a congregation of two hundred and fifty. A goal must be challenging. Never become content with the status quo.

Dr. David Yonggi Cho, retired pastor of the world's largest church, knows the importance of setting challenging faith goals. He started with a faith goal to reach two people with the Gospel. Then after reaching it, he set a more challenging faith goal of five-hundred, then one-thousand, then five-thousand, then ten-thousand and so on. The last I heard, Dr. Cho's church had grown beyond eight hundred thousand members! He kept challenging himself with bigger faith goals. God gave Dr. Cho the results because this man dared to set challenging goals and persevered to move ahead in accomplishing them. To be effective, goals must be challenging.

6. Your faith goals should be somewhat realistic.

I wouldn't recommend setting a goal to "sell a thousand insurance policies this week," if you have never even sold twenty policies in a week. And please don't set a goal to "create a new planet" if you don't have the faith to create a new planet (which you don't). Pastor, don't set a goal to "gain five-thousand church members within a year" if your church size is now only one hundred members. Be somewhat realistic! Take incremental steps. Don't go ridiculously beyond your faith or your God-given abilities. Set challenging, but realistic, ten-year faith goals, five-year faith goals, two-year faith goals, one-year faith goals, six-month faith goals, three-month faith goals, etc. Break your larger faith goals down into smaller faith goals.

Make your faith goals big, leaving room for God to work miracles, but don't bring reproach upon your faith by setting your faith goals way beyond your current level of faith. Dr. Cho did not start out with a goal to win two hundred thousand people in one year. He started with a realistic goal that challenged his faith level at the time. So the sixth goal-setting rule is to be realistic—challenging, but realistic.

7. Your faith goal should include a deadline.

Until you set a target date for its accomplishment, your goal will be more like a vague wish—something you hope to do eventually. Can you imagine planning your wedding but setting no date? The bride would go crazy. How about planning a vacation with no dates? It doesn't make any sense at all. The same is true if you set a faith goal with no deadline.

The late Zig Ziglar once said, "A goal casually set and lightly taken, will be freely abandoned at the first obstacle." This explains why New Year's resolutions rarely work. I say, "Don't make New Year's resolutions; instead make fresh faith goals for the year."

Most of us work better under a little pressure, and deadlines help provide the needed pressure to spur us on until the goal or task is accomplished.

Ask yourself, "What are the desirable target dates for accomplishing each step of this project?" Then set realistic deadlines. A goal isn't really a goal until it is assigned a deadline. Target dates, or deadlines, will help you schedule your time better and also will provide a means of checking your progress.

When I set a goal for my ministry to go on the radio with the *Good Ground Faith-Building Broadcast*, my team and I also set a time schedule. We planned the date to begin recording. Then we set a target date to go on the air. My team and I made our plans prayerfully, counting on God to direct us, and with his help we met our deadlines.

Now, suppose you establish no deadlines. You could say, "Oh well, I'll probably start next week." With no concrete deadlines, it's easy to put things off or try to make things perfect before starting. But there is a universal law at work here: *Work expands to fill the time available for its completion.* In other words, if you set an open-ended goal, your work will keep increasing to fill the time available for its completion. Since there is no deadline, the faith goal cannot be accomplished. This is the so-called Parkinson's Law.[1]

> **If you wait for the perfect conditions, you will never get anything done.**
> **Ecclesiastes 11:4 TLB**

When a goal has no deadline, we have a tendency to wait for perfect conditions. For example, if I had no target date for the completion of this book, I would revise it non-stop, search for all the grammatical errors in it, and change things around continuously. Every day I would think of something else to improve; perhaps another chapter, maybe some better illustrations and examples, or perhaps I'd change the chapter titles or wait until I came up with a better name for the book. It would most likely take men99 years to refine, revise, re-edit, and redo this book. In other words, it would never get published if I waited until everything about it was perfect.

In my ministry, there are certain goals for every department. The departmental leaders are responsible for setting goals and deadlines within the framework of our larger corporate goals. They are encouraged to find creative ways of reaching these goals. They set target dates. Each month, progress is evaluated

---

[1] Parkinson, C. Northcote; *Parkinson's Law: or The Law of Progress*, Penguin Books, New York, NY, 1957.

and recorded for each department. This gives us an adequate means of measuring our progress.

GOD WORKS BY SCHEDULES

God set a time schedule for creation. Read the first chapter of Genesis. God worked and created according to his time schedule.

The Messiah, Jesus Christ, came to earth right on schedule. He rode into Jerusalem on the colt of a donkey the exact day God said he would.[2]

God has a time schedule for the return of Jesus. By the signs all around us, I would say we are getting close to this deadline being met. I pray that you have made your peace with God.[3]

When you set your goals and make your plans, don't fail to set a time schedule. And be realistic yet challenging enough to make room for God's miracles.

MISTAKES IN SETTING FAITH GOALS

1. **Setting faith goals too low.** This leaves no room for miracles. Goals that are easily achieved cause us to lose our excitement and enthusiasm quickly. There is nothing in setting low goals to stir our blood.

2. **Setting faith goals too high.** This may cause feelings of discouragement and defeat. You may be tempted to quit altogether when you realize your goal was not realistically achievable.

3. **Not understanding that faith goals must be set higher as they are attained.** Goals are only temporary resting points. As you accomplish one

[2] Daniel 9:24–26
[3] Matthew 24; Mark 13; Luke 21

goal, prayerfully establish a new one just a little more challenging. There is another universal law that every successful person knows: *Unless you continue to grow, expand, and develop, you will level off and die.*

HOW TO SET FAITH GOALS AND ACHIEVE THEM

1. **See in your inner eye the overall dream.**
2. **Prayerfully establish goals by faith.** Consider whether or not the goal will move you forward to achieving the vision.
3. **Develop a plan for reaching the faith goal.** Include target dates and smaller steps you must take to achieve the completion of your faith goal. Develop your plan with details.
4. **Build a team.** Gather people around you who share your vision and are willing to help you.
5. **Always move on your own initiative.** Once God helps you establish a faith goal, don't wait for the right mood or feeling. Paul told Timothy to "stir up" his gift. Those who wait for the right mood to pray, seldom pray. People who stall until the inspiration comes usually accomplish nothing of lasting value.
6. **Move ahead with great perseverance.** There will be obstacles to overcome, but you can do it with God's help. Remember, Jesus is *always* with you. "

Faithful is He that calleth you, who also will do it.
1 Thessalonians 5:24

You will face obstacles, roadblocks, and challenges. One purpose of these types of obstacles is to make us stop relying on ourselves and learn to rely on God. So, plan for obstacles.

> ³ **A prudent person foresees danger and takes precautions. The simpleton goes blindly on and suffers the consequences.**
>
> ⁴ **True humility and fear of the Lord lead to riches, honor, and long life.**
>
> **Proverbs 22:3–4 NLT**

I love verse four in this Proverb, "True humility and fear of the Lord lead to riches, honor, and a long life." When you set faith goals that are too big to achieve without God's help, it keeps you humble. The kind of true humility that leads to riches, honor, and a long life is when you put your hand in God's hand, and ask him to help you every step of the way.

FIVE REASONS WHY PEOPLE DON'T SET FAITH GOALS

1. **They don't know how.**
2. **They are lazy.** They think it's too much trouble to set faith goals.
3. **They believe contrary teaching about goals.**
4. **They don't have faith.** They don't believe that God will help them accomplish their goals.
5. **They are cynical.** They've set long-term goals in the past and didn't see immediate results so they give up and become cynical.

In review, the necessary steps to planning are:

- **First, define your dream.**
- **Second, you must set faith goals and deadlines.**

IT'S MORE ABOUT WHAT YOU ARE BECOMING THAN WHAT YOU ARE GETTING

Faith goals will do something in you. It's not about what you get; it's about what you are becoming. And faith goals help you become something more on the inside so you can enjoy more on the outside. I don't want you to be like the Beatles' *Nowhere Man*. I want to see you charged with faith and vision, hope and dreams, and written faith goals. Faith goals will transform your life like nothing you can imagine.

I have an expensive leather notebook I call "Dave's Faith Goals." I put a picture of me on the front of that book. And in it I've pasted pictures from magazines—things that speak to my vision. And then every time I plant a seed, I always believe God for a harvest. If you look at my harvest list, and you look at my faith goals list, they will always coincide. I encourage you to get a book just for setting faith goals.

God himself set faith goals. He set deadlines. "Jesus is going to be born here. He is going to be crucified there. He is going to be raised from the dead here. He's going to ascend to heaven there, and the church is going to do this in this period of time...." And then, God has a faith goal that only he knows. Only he knows the day and the hour when Jesus is going to come back. God always works from a plan.

Now, lets you and I be twined together with God in covenant through Jesus, and set and reach faith goals for our lives, our families, our ministries, our businesses, and become a thousand times more!

> **The Lord God of your fathers make you a thousand times so many more as ye are, and bless you, as he hath promised you!**
>
> **Deuteronomy 1:11**

My Prayer for You

I pray that for you, my brother, my sister. I pray that God will enlighten your heart and advance your plans and dreams. I pray he will pour awesome vision into your heart and mind during your times of intimacy with him. I pray that you get the real sense that Jesus is working with you, twined together to help you reach your greatest potential in him, to catapult your vision and your dreams into reality. I pray that all the promises of God will become provisions in your life. I pray this for you, my friend, in Jesus' Name.   Amen!"

Next we'll discuss the V5 stage of the planning process. Having read this chapter on goals, you have no excuse for not sitting down TODAY and prayerfully setting your own faith goals. Don't settle for a run-of-the-mill existence. Set your faith goals now, and let God lift you to new heights of achievement.

PRINCIPLES IN REVIEW

The seven fundamental goal-setting rules:

1. A faith goal must be specific.
2. You should prayerfully set your own faith goals.
3. Your faith goals should take you closer to fulfilling your life's dream.
4. Your faith goals should be written down.
5. Your faith goals should be challenging.
6. Your faith goals should be somewhat realistic.
7. Your faith goals should include a deadline.

V1 **Values:** Stemming from God's Word

V2 **Vision:** Your General Concept, Dream, or Desire

V3 **Voicing:** Making Your Faith Forecast

V4 **Vividness:** Setting Faith Goals, Plans, Organizing

V5 **Visioning:** Seeing it in Your Inner Person in Detail

V6 **Vitalizing:** Bringing Life to Faith Goals by Action

V7 **Victory:** Seeing Your Dream Realized

CHAPTER 8

PRODUCING YOUR
OWN FAITH MOVIE

In the previous chapters we looked at the first four phases in the **V7 Strategy** planning process: **V1**: values; **V2**: vision (defining your dream); V3: making faith forecasts; and **V4**: establishing faith goals and deadlines. We now come to the **V5** stage: visioning or producing faith movies!

As I previously stated, vision (V2), is a comprehensive sense of where you are now and where you are going. It's the big picture of something in your future. It's a concept of where you are headed.

Visioning (V5) is different. Visioning is like producing a faith movie in your mind and heart. You see it in prayer. You see it on the inside of you. It's a form of meditation based on God's script (Scriptures, promises, and instructions).

This Book of the Law shall not depart out of your mouth, but you shall meditate on it day and night, that you may observe and do according to all that

is written in it. For then you shall make your way prosperous, and then you shall deal wisely and have good success.

Joshua 1:8 AMP

I will meditate also of all thy work, and talk of thy doings.

Psalm 77:12

In our faith forecasting, faith goal setting, and faith movie producing, we do not put human limits on our dreams and goals. We meditate on God, his Word, and his power to help us achieve what seems impossible. In a faith movie, we use our faith, our mind, and our imagination to meditate on the possibilities beyond human possibilities.

Jesus looked at them intently and said, "Humanly speaking, it is impossible. But with God everything is possible."

Matthew 19:26 NLT

And Jesus looking upon them saith, With men it is impossible, but not with God: for with God all things are possible.

Mark 10:27

HOW TO REACH YOUR FAITH GOALS

As a believer, you should never attempt to set or accomplish great goals in the natural energy of the flesh. This is futile and frustrating. Those who would do the work of God in the energy of the flesh will eventually feel the effects and stresses of today's high-pressure living.

This is a problem. Many are trying to reach lofty goals by making promises, striving, pushing, and overworking. For instance, many sincere Christians are trying to reach a goal of righteousness by struggling for it. They don't seem to realize that Jesus Christ paid the price for our righteousness.[1] *Our righteousness is his righteousness and his righteousness is our righteousness.* It doesn't seem like a fair trade, since our righteousness is really nothing but filthy rags in the sight of God. But our God made the covenant with us, and we must accept, by imputation, the righteousness of Jesus Christ upon our lives. That means we have faith that Jesus traded his holiness and righteousness for our sin and guilt as a free gift to us. There is no more struggling, only faith. St. Paul said to the Galatians,

> **Are ye so foolish? having begun in the Spirit, are ye now made perfect by the flesh?**
>
> **Galatians 3:3**

Even as true righteousness, acceptable in God's sight, cannot be realized by human effort, so it is with God-given faith goals. They can only be achieved by trusting in the Holy Spirit's guidance, help, and strength. Zerubbabel, the priest, was faced with an enormous task and wondered how it could ever be accomplished. God's answer came to him…

> **"Not by might, nor by power, but by my Spirit, saith the Lord of hosts."**
>
> **Zechariah 4:6**

We must learn to depend upon the Holy Spirit and his power when desiring to reach our challenging goals.

FAITH MOVIES

After establishing your faith goals, you must, in your prayers and thoughts, produce a faith movie of yourself successfully

---

[1] Romans 5:17; 1Corinthians 1:20; Galatians 2:21; Philippians 3:9

103

reaching the goals and deadlines. Just picture Jesus standing beside you, helping you, and guiding you. He said in Hebrews 13:5, "I'll never leave you nor forsake you. I'll be with you even unto the end of the age."

Have you ever known anyone who wanted to lose weight? I have known people who had a *desire* to lose several pounds, *believed* they could do it with God's help, *studied how* to lose weight, *set their goals*, and then placed a picture of an enormously obese person on the refrigerator door thinking it would deter them from overeating. Quite frankly, I do not favor this method. I believe that when you pray in faith, you should *see* the answer to your prayers through your eyes of faith. Looking at a picture of an overweight person sets you to thinking in terms of fat, and automatically you find yourself hungry all the time. Subconsciously your system is trying to make you into what you are picturing in your mind's eye.

A couple of years back, I set a goal to lose thirty pounds of undesirable fat. I didn't produce a faith movie of myself getting fatter. That wouldn't have been faith. I asked for God's help, and therefore I saw myself in my faith movie getting thinner. Before long the extra thirty pounds were gone!

IF YOU ARE WILLING TO "SEE" IT ON THE INSIDE, YOU CAN HAVE IT ON THE OUTSIDE

Your inner kingdom becomes your outer kingdom. Your inner reality will become your outer reality

> For as he thinks in his heart, so is he.
>
> Proverbs 23:7a AMP

In this step, you produce a faith movie of your vision and each of your faith goals, using God's promises as the script for your movie.

After articulating your vision and setting a faith goal toward realizing it, see yourself in a faith movie reaching it. Don't think in terms of failure. Picturing failure produces fear, and fear hinders your faith. You need faith to reach your goal. Picture yourself reaching your faith goal as God helps you.

In Judges 6:12, we find the Lord trying to get Gideon to see a faith movie of himself as a mighty warrior by actually calling him one. Later, in Judges 6:34–35, we find Gideon *actually becoming* a mighty warrior. A spiritual law was in action—FAITH MOVIES! We attract to ourselves that which we see with our eyes of faith.

God showed Abraham the stars of heaven and told him that his offspring would be as numerous. This *seemed* impossible from a natural standpoint, since Abraham and his wife were both very old—Sarah was *far* past the age of reproduction—and had no children. But every time Abraham looked up at the stars at night he would—in his mind and in his spirit—remember God's promise. Then it happened! A miracle! Though impossible in the natural, Sarah gave birth to a baby boy, and through this child Abraham eventually became the father of many nations. Abraham produced his own faith movie. When he looked at those stars, he saw himself as the father of many nations, and it came to pass!

When I first became a Christian, I started producing faith movies of myself as a preacher of God's Word. I'd see myself before hundreds of people, sharing the Good News of Jesus Christ. As I prayed, I would use this remarkable spiritual law. I remember practicing my sermons and *picturing* myself in the pulpit. I went over every detail in my mind and could literally *feel* myself being used of God in this capacity.

Without any human effort, pushing, or scheming for an opportunity, I soon found myself doing the very things I had *seen* in my faith movies. The pastor of one of the largest churches in the community asked me to come and preach. In a matter of months, I was preaching to hundreds, just as I had pictured, and I have been ever since!

One of the leading evangelists in the country used this process of *producing* faith movies. As a boy, he would go to an old, closed-down root beer stand and preach his heart out. He would preach and preach and preach! Of course nobody was there, but he'd still preach and picture thousands of people listening and responding to the message. He would think about what his grandmother had once told him, "Someday you'll be preaching to thousands of people." He meditated upon those words. He saw them coming true in his faith movie. And today he is not only preaching to thousands, but millions! This is another clear indication of the effectiveness of the spiritual practice of producing faith movies.

CANCER HEALED

Harry was diagnosed with terminal cancer and was sent home to die. One day, he received a Christian magazine in the mail that contained an article about a woman who had been healed by the power of her faith in God. This got Harry to thinking...*is there really power in faith?*

Soon he began to pray with childlike faith. As a result of his prayers, God gave him a heaven-sent idea: *begin to picture the healthy white cells in your body marching to battle against the unhealthy cells.* So Harry did this several times a day, praying, believing, and producing this faith movie.

One day he noticed that he was hungry when before he had no appetite at all. He began to eat with a good appetite and started feeling much better. After many weeks, his astonished doctors told Harry that the disease was gone—in remission. Harry became a healthy man!

A BARREN WOMAN MADE FRUITFUL

Elisha, the prophet, told a barren woman that she would be embracing a child by the next year. Why do you suppose he used the word *embracing* instead of just telling her she would become pregnant and give birth to a child? Do you think perhaps it was because it's so much more vivid for a person to *picture* something specific—like, "holding a child," than it is to picture something as abstract as merely "having a baby?" Of course! She probably thought often about holding—embracing—that little child, *seeing* his little face in her faith movie, talking and singing to the little fellow.

Even though it was difficult for her to believe, she could still hope and watch her self-produced faith movie. As she did, her hope turned to faith and was released to God. Then, sure enough, a miracle took place and Elisha's prophesy came true!

> **¹⁶ And he said, about this season, according to the time of life, thou shalt embrace a son. And she said, Nay, my Lord, though man of God, do not lie unto thine handmaid.**
>
> **¹⁷ And the woman conceived and bare a son at the season that Elisha had said unto her, according to the time of life.**
>
> **2 Kings 4:16–17**

EVANGELISM

Jesus said,

> **Lift up your eyes and *look* on the fields; for they are white already to harvest.**
>
> **John 4:35b (italics added)**

In this verse, wasn't he seeking to get his disciples to see a faith movie of something of vast importance? He wanted them to *picture* every one of those stalks of wheat as a human being, ready to be harvested into the family of God, ready to be reached with the Gospel of the Kingdom. "Behold, today is the day...." Don't wait. Get out there and start reaching the lost. Pray that the Lord of the harvest will send laborers into the harvest.

Every time you go by a wheat field, picture yourself as a great soul winner, a harvester. Picture yourself leading people to Jesus Christ as easily as a farmer would harvest his wheat. Don't picture leading only one or two to God (as good as that is), but produce a faith movie with yourself as a farmer, harvesting thousands of stalks; leading scores of people to a saving knowledge of Jesus Christ. With a full, ripe harvest do you think that a farmer would be satisfied to harvest only one or two stalks of wheat? No, he would not be satisfied with that. He wants to harvest *every* stalk! And he expects to get it!

Jesus was trying to get us to think BIG; to produce big faith movies of huge accomplishments. There is a great power available to the person who will learn to mentally and spiritually, in prayer, produce faith movies.

BEWARE OF HARMFUL MOVIES

Producing faith movies is a form of meditation as described in the Bible. It can be used for our good, or it can be used for our detriment. That is why the psalmist said,

> Let the words of my mouth, and the meditation of my heart, be acceptable in thy sight, O Lord, my strength and my redeemer.
>
> **Psalm 19:14**

Let's look at some of the incorrect uses of this principle. Worry is a form of a mental movie. However, it is not a helpful, positive movie. It is a negative, horror movie. Worry focuses on future trouble—real or imagined. This type of movie is not pleasing to God because it demonstrates a lack of trust in his promises.

The devil knows the power of faith movies. Therefore, he tries to get this law to work against you. That's why he keeps producing pornographic material, health scares, and fabricated bad news about recession, depression, wars, and rumors of wars. If he can get you to *focus* on things that pollute your mind and cripple your creative abilities, he will have accomplished his purpose, and you will fall short of reaching your God-directed goals.

It's simple. If you see failure in your faith movie, you will fail. If you see yourself falling short of your faith goal, you probably will. But if you picture yourself reaching your faith goals, with God helping you, regardless of the number of problems or setbacks that may be involved, *you will achieve success.* You may experience a delay or a detour from time to time, but eventually your dream will become a reality.

After setting your faith goals, picture them already in existence...now! The Bible says, "NOW faith is."[2] Establish a faith-image, a faith movie, of your accomplished goal. Remember, real faith "calls those things which are not as though they already are."[3]

Before I ever wrote my first book, *Success Principles from the Lips of Jesus*, I had the artwork for the cover drawn up. It was just a rough sketch but suitable for my purpose. Then I prayed and began to picture the book already completed and published. Every time I'd walk into my office, there was the sketch of the front cover of my book. I set up a faith-image and began to see the finished work with my eyes of faith. Soon everything within me began to press toward the goal. Sentence after sentence, chapter

---

[2] Hebrews 11:1
[3] Romans 4:17

109

after chapter, I worked, prayed, and watched my own faith movie. Within one year, God honored my faith and crowned my efforts with success! I published my first book!

DON'T GET DISCOURAGED

Do not allow yourself to get discouraged if you don't know exactly how you will reach your goal. You simply pray and **picture** the end results. God will give you heaven-sent ideas when you need them. Sometimes God purposely withholds the "how to" information up front to ensure you continue to seek him throughout the process.

Don't worry. God will send people, or even angels if necessary, to help you reach your goals. But you must use the process of establishing a faith-image, or see a faith movie, of the end result of your faith goal.

What is your vision? Have you articulated it through a faith forecast? Have you made it vivid with your faith goals? Can you see it now in your faith movie?

V1 **Values:** Stemming from God's Word

V2 **Vision:** Your General Concept, Dream, or Desire

V3 **Voicing:** Making Your Faith Forecast

V4 **Vividness:** Setting Faith Goals, Plans, Organizing

V5 **Visioning:** Seeing it in Your Inner Person in Detail

V6 **Vitalizing:** Bringing Life to Faith Goals by Action

V7 **Victory:** Seeing Your Dream Realized

CHAPTER 9

FAITH SEES THE END RESULT

Faith sees things that others do not see. Some people might say faith is blind. That is incorrect. The person with faith sees things that are unseen to the person without faith.

> **If people can't see what God is doing, they stumble all over themselves;**
>
> **But when they attend to what he reveals, they are most blessed.**
>
> **Proverbs 29:18 MSG**

There are critics of this message. I realize that. They can complain and criticize all they want. But you will notice something very interesting: Men and women who have achieved great things for God's glory have always been men and women of character, men and women of *vision*, men and women who have, in one way or another, learned to establish faith goals and produce their own faith movies.

On the other hand, look at the accomplishments of the critics. Quite often you'll find that they have made very little progress of any lasting value to the Kingdom of God. The success they have achieved is usually at the cost of hindering the faith of some of God's precious children. You can be above that by being open to God's Spirit as he reveals God's will for your life. Then start seeing the end result of your goal in your faith movie.

SEE IT!

See a faith movie of success, not failure. Meditate upon God's Word, not the word of the world. Picture yourself reaching your goal, not falling short. Envision God's Spirit opening the right doors at the right time in the right way. Don't envision yourself beating your head against a stone wall. Write a movie with a victorious ending not a tragic ending.

Remember, it's almost impossible to produce genuine faith-filled movies and continue to get the wrong results. The most important things in your heart and mind will have a tendency to come to pass, whether good or bad.[1] You will attract to yourself what you see in your faith movie. Once again, it's because your inner reality tends to become your outer reality.

Why is that difficult to understand? We know that a person must first accept an inner reality by receiving Jesus Christ before their outer reality really changes.

> [12] **But as many as received him, to them gave he power to become the sons of God, even to them that believe on his name:**
>
> [13] **Which were born, not of blood, nor of the will of the flesh, nor of the will of man, but of God.**
>
> **John 1:12–13**

---

[1] Proverbs 23:7; Mark 7:20–23; Philippians 4:7–9; Psalm 101:3

¹⁷ **This means that anyone who belongs to Christ has become a new person. The old life is gone; a new life has begun!**

¹⁸ **And all of this is a gift from God, who brought us back to himself through Christ. And God has given us this task of reconciling people to him.**

¹⁹ **For God was in Christ, reconciling the world to himself, no longer counting people's sins against them. And he gave us this wonderful message of reconciliation.**

2 Corinthians 5:17–19 NLT

The inner reality comes first, then the outer reality begins to harmonize from one glorious step to another.[2]

THE MIRACLE STARTS ON THE INSIDE

The miracle is born on the inside first, then the miracle continues to develop by making new things and fresh changes on the outside. It's the same with reaching your faith goals and producing your faith movies. A faith picture must be projected on your mind's inner screen before it can manifest on the outside.

This is true and simple: **Faith sees the end result.**

YOUR PRAYER-DREAM BOOK

Again, I want to encourage you to get a notebook and write out your faith goals. I like to cut out pictures from magazines that illustrate a particular faith goal. For instance, if my faith goal is to move my family into a new home, I look for pictures of how I would like the house to look—pictures of a great kitchen, a cozy living room, etc. If I read an article that inspires me regarding one of my faith goals, I cut it out and put it in my notebook. When I am studying my Bible, I look for God's

---

[2] 2 Corinthians 3:18

promises that speak to my faith goals and write them into my notebook. Find creative ways to make each faith goal you set more concrete—easier for your picture to come true.

Once you establish a general vision or dream, set smaller faith goals that will move you toward achievement. As you complete each smaller faith goal, check it off and celebrate your success. As you do, you will find yourself attaining higher and higher levels of success and accomplishment.

1. Write down your spiritual faith goals.
2. Write down your personal faith goals.
3. Write down your family faith goals.
4. Write down your ministry faith goals.
5. Write down your professional and career faith goals.
6. Write down your financial faith goals.
7. From your list of goals, pick **one** from each category and concentrate your efforts on reaching it.
8. Set a deadline for each faith goal.
9. Make a list of the things you'd like to accomplish in the next few months.
10. From your list, pick **one** as your primary current faith goal.
11. List one progressive step you are going to take to start achieving your faith goals in each category.
12. Where do you want to be five years from now?
13. What are your greatest strengths and God-given talents? How do you plan to build on them?
14. Have you gained the self-respect that comes from knowing you are doing the very best you can, and trusting God to do the rest?

Setting faith goals is something failures don't do. Failing businesses, failing churches, failing people, and failing relationships are often the result of never setting progressive faith goals for growth, expansion, and development.

SETTING FAITH GOALS

1. List any obstacles you may face in reaching this faith goal.
2. Devise a plan for dealing with the obstacles.
3. List any people, groups, or organizations that may be able to help you reach this faith goal.
4. List any skills or knowledge you will need to achieve this faith goal.
5. List the benefits you'll receive from accomplishing this faith goal.
6. Give the faith goal a deadline; a target date for completion.
7. List all the Scriptures and Bible promises you'll need in order to fulfill this faith goal.
8. Build in reserves (time, money, and people).
9. Make all your faith goals harmonize with one another.
10. Write out a clear, concise plan of action and move ahead with perseverance.

Solomon said, "There is a time to be born, and a time to die." That is certainly true. But what you accomplish between those two points is up to you! Set your faith goals and reach them! Articulate your dream, make your faith forecast, set your faith goals, produce your faith movie...and let the adventure begin!

PRINCIPLES IN REVIEW:

1. *Never* attempt to accomplish great goals in the natural energy of the flesh.
2. If you can *see it* on the inside, you can eventually *have it* on the outside!
3. After setting a goal, produce a *faith movie* of yourself where you have already reached it.
4. *Faith movies* can have a beneficial effect or a detrimental effect depending on your focus.
5. If your *faith movies* focus on failure, you will fail!
6. Faith sees things that others do not see.
7. The focus of your faith movie will attract that reality to your life.

V1 **Values:** Stemming from God's Word

V2 **Vision:** Your General Concept, Dream, or Desire

V3 **Voicing:** Making Your Faith Forecast

V4 **Vividness:** Setting Faith Goals, Plans, Organizing

V5 **Visioning:** Seeing it in Your Inner Person in Detail

V6 **Vitalizing:** Bringing Life to Faith Goals by Action

V7 **Victory:** Seeing Your Dream Realized

10

VITALIZING YOUR DREAM

In this chapter, we are going to take action. "V6" is the stage where you will vitalize your vision by taking action on your faith goals. Remember, faith goals are micro-steps that carry you closer to realizing your vision. Faith—true faith—is active.

THIS IS A PRIORITY

This is more important than doing the dishes or laundry.

This is more important than shopping or rushing off to a sale.

This is more important than making the golf tee time.

This is more important than answering the telephone and will have greater value.

This one practice can bring an extravagant and profound expansion to your future success.

> **For as the body without the spirit is dead, so faith without works is dead also.**
>
> **James 2:26**

Faith without action is dead. Action is the key that vitalizes—brings to life—your dream.

> **A life frittered away disgusts God; he loves those who run straight for the finish line.**
>
> **Proverbs 15:9 MSG**

> **Commit your actions to the Lord, and your plans will succeed.**
>
> **Proverbs 16:3 NLT**

High achievers know that they can have an entire encyclopedia of plans, faith goals, and dreams but only faith actions will vitalize them. Life springs forth to your dreams and faith goals after you take that first step. A ten-foot thick book of faith goals is worthless if you don't act on them. Take that first step now. *Execute your plan.*

TAKING ACTION NOW

Let's start taking some action now. Here's what I'd like you to do:

1. Set aside a ten to twelve hour block of time to be alone. Take nothing but your Bible, a notebook and pen—or if you prefer, use your computer. You and your spouse may also do this together, although sometimes it is better to do it separately, and then schedule a time together to mesh your goals, eliminate some, and determine the top priority goals.

2. Decide exactly what you want in every area of life. This may take a few hours, but the Lord encourages us to desire "things" and talk with him about it.

> **Therefore I say unto you, What *things* soever ye desire, when ye pray, believe that ye receive them, and ye shall have them.**
>
> **Mark 11:24 (italics added)**

Project yourself ahead 10 years. How do you see yourself (or your church, ministry, or business, etc.)?

Cover the most important areas of your life. Your extraordinary future depends on this. Beside each area of life where you wrote your faith goals, ask the question, "Why do I want to see this faith goal become a reality?" Crystallize your thoughts regarding why you want it, what the purpose is behind it.

IGNITE YOUR MOTIVATION WITH THE "WHY"

The "why?" must be meaningful to you. For instance, if you desire an investment account of $800,000, your reason (your why?) may be to send your children or grandchildren to college, to dress better, to live better, to be able to give more to God's work. Whatever your "why?" is, it must have a strong importance, value, and relevance to you.

When the why is strong, it will ignite motivation and increase your chances of success. You have to know why achieving this goal is important to you. A goal without a supporting purpose will not have as much power to pull you toward achieving the goal.

- **Spiritually**
- **Intellectually**
- **Relationally**
- **Financially**
- **Physically**
- **Recreationally**
- **Materially**
- **Educationally**
- **Professionally**

3. Ask yourself the question, "Are these dreams and goals flowing from my chief values? Are there promises in God's Word I can stand upon in the realization of my dreams?"

4. Write out your faith goal clearly and specifically, calling those things that are not as though they already are. This is faith forecasting—voicing your vision. Always write it down on paper!

5. Begin speaking aloud those things that are not yet visible as if they were already here. See it. Speak it. Believe it, and thank God for it.

> **…God, who quickeneth the dead, and calleth those things which be not as though they were.**
> **Romans 4:17**

6. Set a target date for your dream to be realized, and set sub-target dates for your faith goals. This is to ensure your progress along the way. God knew the exact target date he had planned for Jesus to come.

> **But when the fulness of the time was come, God sent forth his Son….**
> **Galatians 4:4**

7. List the things you may need in order to reach your faith goal.

> **¹ Solomon decided to build a Temple to honor the name of the LORD, and also a royal palace for himself.**
> **² He enlisted a force of 70,000 laborers, 80,000 men to quarry stone in the hill country, and 3,600 foremen.**

> [3] Solomon also sent this message to King Hiram at Tyre: "Send me cedar logs as you did for my father, David, when he was building his palace.
>
> [4] I am about to build a Temple to honor the name of the LORD my God...."
>
> 2 Chronicles 2:1–4 a NLT

> So Solomon began to build the Temple of the LORD in Jerusalem on Mount Moriah, where the LORD had appeared to David, his father.
>
> 2 Chronicles 3:1

Answer these questions:

- What kind of person will I need to become in order to reach my goals?
- What education or research must I complete to reach my goals? What courses, classes, or mentoring will I require?
- What associations will I need to make or nurture in order to achieve my goals?
- What associations will I need to limit or dismiss in order to achieve my goals?
- What will I need to start doing in order to achieve my goals?
- What will I need to stop doing in order to achieve my goals?

8. Organize your list into a plan with a schedule and priorities. Remember, God also works by schedules. Think of his plan and schedule for Creation: Day 1, Day 2, etc.

> David organized his forces. He appointed captains of thousands and captains of hundreds.
>
> 2 Samuel 18:1

125

9. Take an action immediately.

> **What good is it, dear brothers and sisters, if you say you have faith but don't show it by your actions?**
>
> **James 2:14 NLT**

> **How foolish! Can't you see that faith without good deeds is useless?**
>
> **James 2:20 NLT**

10. Do something every day toward your key faith goals.

> **The LORD will make you successful in your daily work.**
>
> **Deuteronomy 28:6 CEV**

You may download free V7 Faith Goals Forms by visiting: www.faithgoalsbook.com.

MIRACLE-IZE YOUR LIFE WITH THE V7 STRATEGY

You may think you are starting all of this with "nothing." If that's the case, use your faith as the substance and evidence of what you hope for—your vision.

> **[1] Now faith is the substance of things hoped for, the evidence of things not seen.**
> **[2] For by it the elders obtained a good report.**
> **[3] Through faith we understand that the worlds were framed by the word of God, so that things which are seen were not made of things which do appear.**
>
> **Hebrews 11:1–3**

Notice in verse 3 we are told, "...things which are seen were not made of things which do appear." In other words, you won't see the vision in the natural realm at first, so you must see it in the spiritual realm by faith. Everything you now see was made from substance you cannot see.

It sounds strange but even Jesus told us that it is the invisible that moves the visible.

> ⁵⁻⁶ Jesus said, "You're not listening. Let me say it again. Unless a person submits to this original creation—the 'wind-hovering-over-the-water' creation, *the invisible moving the visible*, a baptism into a new life—it's not possible to enter God's kingdom. When you look at a baby, it's just that: a body you can look at and touch. But the person who takes shape within is formed by something you can't see and touch—the Spirit—and becomes a living spirit.
>
> John 3:5–6 MSG (italics added)

Look at things that cannot be seen in the natural realm. You can begin to fulfill a dream even when you start with nothing. Of course, since the invisible moves the visible, and faith is an actual substance, you can't really call it nothing. But if you are starting with no money, no support, no plan, no resources, you can still bring a vision out of the invisible realm and make it a visible reality.

> While we look not at the things which are seen, but at the things which are not seen: for the things which are seen are temporal; but the things which are not seen are eternal.
>
> 2 Corinthians 4:18

Jesus commands you to lift up your eyes and see what others don't see or what others refuse to see.

> Say not ye, There are yet four months, and then cometh harvest? behold, I say unto you, Lift up your eyes, and look on the fields; for they are white already to harvest.
>
> John 4:35

SEEING THE INVISIBLE TO SHAPE THE VISIBLE

When I was pastor of a 125 member church, I saw it as having 1,000 members. As I would pray in the early hours, I would close my eyes and see the vision of a thousand members. Within a few years, we were holding five Sunday services to accommodate all the worshippers. When we hit 1,000, I saw 3,000. I then saw daughter churches that did not yet exist. But over the next 15 years, 43 daughter churches were established

Top: Mount Hope Church in Lansing, Michigan
Bottom: Two of our Daughter Churches in Gaylord and Corunna, Michigan. We now have over 500 Mount Hope Churches in America, Africa, and Asia.

with pastors we trained, and over 500 more in Africa and Asia, totaling a membership of over 80,000 worshippers! Think of it: from 125 to over 80,000 by using the V7 Faith Goals Strategy.

> **...God who brings the dead back to life and who creates new things out of nothing.**
>
> **Romans 4:17 NLT**

> **... God, who quickeneth the dead, and calleth those things which be not as though they were.**
>
> **Romans 4:17**

Up to this point, it's been more theory than practice. Now, let's look at the V7 Strategy in a practical way.

SAMPLE V7 STRATEGY

Here's a sample:

- **MY VISION:** I see myself healthy and fit, well groomed, and well dressed, whether I'm casual or dressed up for an event.
- **VALUE:** Under "Fitness"
- **WHY?** (Remember the why may have stronger force than the what when writing your vision and faith goals). **I have this vision because my body is the Temple of the Holy Spirit.** I will be an inspiration to others, will live a long, fruitful life, enjoy my family and friends, and have fun with them. I will travel in good health as I carry the message of Christ's love.
- **Faith Goal 1: Lose 20 pounds**
  My action plan for Faith Goal 1:

- ▸ Get a book on good nutrition and study it.

- ▸ Set caloric/carbohydrate/fat intake per day.

- ▸ Plan meals according to my planned nutrition.

- ▸ Walk 20 minutes a day.

- ▸ Get a personal trainer at the gym.

- **Faith Goal 2: Get Blood Pressure to a Perfect 120/70**

  My action plan for Faith Goal 2:

  - ▸ Get a blood pressure cuff from pharmacy.

  - ▸ Check Blood Pressure at various times daily and record results.

  - ▸ Find a good supplement that helps with blood pressure.

  - ▸ Attend a seminar on how to lower your blood pressure naturally.

- **Faith Goal 3: Get hair cut and styled every three weeks**

  My action plan for Faith Goal 3:

  - ▸ Stop going to the $5 place.

  - ▸ Find a great stylist, even though I may pay more. I'm saving money on food now and can use the savings to patronize a first-class stylist.

  - ▸ Buy good hair products instead of those I've been using from the Dollar Store.

- Faith Goal 4: Read Dr. Don Colbert's book, *Seven Pillars of Health*,[1] and apply the principles.
- When I expect to have achieved this vision: (Date here)

Record Scriptures in your prayer-dream book, or faith goals book as you read God's Word, and write down your prayer thoughts as you talk with God. The Holy Spirit will enlighten your heart to special promises and encouragements as you read. Log them into your prayer-dream book.

Plan your faith goals like you would plan a road trip from Michigan to California. Be specific about when you will stop for the night, how many miles you will drive each day, sights you want to see along the way.

You are going to have a real adventure as you begin the V7 Strategy. But the real delight will be when you see God working on your behalf to bring all your dreams, all his promises and provisions into reality.

---

[1] Colbert, Dr. Don; *Seven Pillars of Health—The Natural Way to Better Health for Life,* Siloam, Division of Charisma House Publishing, Lake Mary, FL, 2006.

V1 **Values:** Stemming from God's Word

V2 **Vision:** Your General Concept, Dream, or Desire

V3 **Voicing:** Making Your Faith Forecast

V4 **Vividness:** Setting Faith Goals, Plans, Organizing

V5 **Visioning:** Seeing it in Your Inner Person in Detail

V6 **Vitalizing:** Bringing Life to Faith Goals by Action

V7 **Victory:** Seeing Your Dream Realized

11
CHAPTER

VICTORY WITH THE V7 STRATEGY

Sit back and ask yourself this question: "What will it be like when this dream comes true?" There's a good chance it will come true when you follow the V7 Strategy. Then you will be saying:

> "See, God has come to save me. I will trust in him and not be afraid. The Lord God is my strength and my song; he has given me victory."
>
> **Isaiah 12:2 NLT**

YOUR DREAM BECOMES REALITY

The V7 final stage is the victory stage. Completion. Success. Victory. You will surely reach this stage as you follow the V7 strategy through all its stages.

For now, relax and dream about what it will be like when you finally reach V7 (victory, success, achievement, accomplishment, attainment) and your dream is a reality.

- Where are you living now?
- What are you driving?
- What kind of schools are your children and grandchildren attending?
- What are you doing for churches and missions?
- Who are you becoming in the process of reaching your faith goals?

I am excited for you. I am thrilled to know that your God-given dreams have, or will soon, come true! I know that God's richest blessings are flowing into your life. Congratulations! Here is my prayer for you...

> *Dear Heavenly Father, please energize this dear one's creativity, and impart big dreams, goals, and plans into this person's life. I pray that you, my dear friend, will experience the joy of setting and reaching your meaningful faith goals. I pray that God will bring you to a place of inner peace, fulfillment, and knowing him intimately as you work together to achieve great dreams. I pray this as a blessing for you, in Jesus' name.*
>
> *Amen.*

Thank you for allowing me to be your coach during your pursuit of the *Miracle of Faith Goals*!

WRITE TO ME

I would love so much to personally be with you on your journey into the realm of vision and faith goals. I'd love to see your progress and share the joy of your achievements. I hope you will write me, visit my web page, or e-mail me.

Dave Williams
P.O. Box 80825
Lansing, MI 48908-0825
dave@davewilliams.com
www.davewilliams.com

If you're ever near an area where we are conducting *The Faith Goals Seminar*, I'd love to meet you in person.

You are going to have fun, and you are going to begin achieving 100 to 1000 times more! Please download my Faith Goal Forms, or you may choose to develop your own. The important thing is to use what works for you.

> **How the king rejoices in your strength, O Lord! He shouts with joy because you give him victory.**
>
> **Psalm 21:1 NLT**

> **I wait quietly before God, for my victory comes from him.**
>
> **Psalm 62:1-3 NLT**

Enjoy your extraordinary life!

FREE DOWNLOADS

For free downloads, please go to: **www.faithgoalsbook.com**

Downloads Include:

- The V7 Strategy
- My List
- Helpful Guidelines
- My Faith Goal
- My Plan...with God's Help

About Dave Williams, D.Min.

America's Pacesetting Life Coach™

Dave is a popular speaker at camps, rallies, minister's conferences, churches, civic group meetings, business training sessions, colleges, and Bible Schools. He coaches church leaders, business leaders, entrepreneurs, and followers of Christ on how to live a pacesetting life. His three-pronged approach—spiritual, attitudinal, and practical—has transformed ordinary people into extraordinarily successful leaders in every field of endeavor.

Through cultivating the individual's inherent gifts and enhancing professional—or ministry—performance, he helps to instill the kind of authentic values that attract success. He emphasizes that staying connected to the Great Commission will ultimately lead to greater levels of accomplishment.

BEST SELLING AUTHOR

Dave has authored over 60 books that teach and inspire readers in Christian growth, financial success, health and healing, and many other areas of Christian living. His book *The New Life...The Start of Something Wonderful* has sold almost three million copies and has been translated into eight languages. More recently, he wrote *The World Beyond* (over

100,000 copies sold). His *Miracle Results of Fasting* (Harrison House Publishers) was an Amazon.com five-star top seller for two years in a row.

Dave's articles and reviews have appeared in national magazines such as *Advance, Pentecostal Evangel, Charisma, Ministries Today, Lansing Magazine, Detroit Free Press, World News*, and others.

Pastoral Ministry

Dave Williams served as pastor of Mount Hope Church in Lansing, Michigan, for more than thirty years. In that time, Dave trained thousands of ministers through the Mount Hope Bible Training Institute, Dave Williams' Church Planter's School, and Dave Williams' School for Pacesetting Church Leaders.

With the help of his staff and partners, Dave established a 72-acre campus with worship center, Bible Training Institute, children's center, Global Prayer Center, Valley of Blessing, Gilead Healing Center, care facilities, event center, café, fitness center, world evangelism headquarters, Global Communications Center, and an office complex with nine buildings.

Church planting and missions have been a focus for Dave Williams. Under his leadership, 43 new Mount Hope Churches were planted in the United States, over 300 in West Africa, South Africa, Zimbabwe, and 200 in Asia with a combined membership exceeding 80,000 people. During Dave's tenure, Mount Hope Church gave over $40,000,000 to world and local missions.

Today, Dave serves as the global ambassador and "Bishop" for Mount Hope Churches. He also leads Strategic Global Mission (for charitable scholarships and grants), Dave Williams Ministries, Club 52 (for business people and entrepreneurs), and The Pacesetting Life Media Ministries.

Dave served as a national general presbyter for the Assemblies of God, assistant district superintendent, executive presbyter, regent for North Central Bible College (now North Central University), and as a national missions board member.

Contact Information

Dave Williams Ministries
P.O. Box 80825
Lansing, MI 48908-0825

For a complete list of Dave Williams'
life-changing books,
audio messages and videos visit our website:

www.davewilliams.com

Or phone:
800-888-7284
or
517-731-0000

About Strategic Global Mission

Strategic Global Mission (SGM) started when Dave and Mary Jo Williams began donating a portion of their salaries to provide scholarships to foreign students who could not afford a quality education in ministry.

In 1987, when they gave their first $300 scholarship to a poor South African student, they had no idea it would evolve into a worldwide charitable ministry that God would use to accelerate the Gospel of Jesus Christ.

That young preacher went out and literally changed the face of God's church throughout South Africa. His simple Gospel message touched the hearts' and minds' of his listeners. The result—thousands of lives were transformed.

Since that time, hundreds of young pastor trainees and church planters have received scholarship money through this charitable outreach. The ministry expanded to also include grants to Christian groups working with at-risk children in inner cities. Hundreds of believers caught the vision and have donated money to SGM earmarked for grants and scholarships.

Now you, too, have an opportunity to take part in this worldwide ministry. You can help provide grants and scholar-ships to men and women who will commit their lives to estab-lishing churches and spreading the Gospel. You can reach out to God's precious children who face so many temptations and snares of the devil every day.

Dave and Mary Jo have seen this ministry make a world of difference, and they are convinced that you will receive God's richest blessings for your generous giving.

Consider becoming a monthly partner with Dave and Mary Jo through Strategic Global Mission. With your scholarship or grant of $300 or your monthly partner gift of $30 you will help accelerate the Gospel of Jesus Christ and save lost souls throughout Africa, Asia, and the Americas.

CONTACT INFORMATION:

Strategic Global Mission
P.O. Box 80825
Lansing, MI 48908-0825
517-731-0000
www.davewilliams.com/sgm

MORE **LIFE CHANGING**
PRODUCTS FROM **DECAPOLIS PUBLISHING**

Shop **decapolisbooks.com** or call 1-800-888-7284